The Story of Street Literature

The Story of Street Literature

Forerunner of the Popular Press
by Robert Collison

Santa Barbara, California   Oxford, England

© 1973
by
Robert Collison

LC Number 72-80716
ISBN 0-87436-094-3
Printed in Great Britain

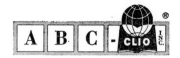

American Bibliographical Center—Clio Press
Riviera Campus, 2040 Alameda Padre Serra
Santa Barbara, California

European Bibliographical Center—Clio Press
30 Cornmarket Street
Oxford OX1 3EY, England

Publisher's Dedication

Charles Folkard, shortly before his death, gave me one of his treasured possessions, a copy of *The Life and Times of James Catnach*. It contained a collection of broadsheets and nursery rhymes that Catnach had published from his press in Seven Dials between 1800 and 1850. They were illustrated with contemporary woodcuts and wood engravings, some by unknown hands and some by artists as famous as Thomas Bewick, who is thought to have worked for the Press at one time. It was these that endeared the book to Charles Folkard, himself a children's book illustrator who achieved great distinction during the first half of this century. When he brought it to me he was kind enough to say that he would like me to have it because he thought I would appreciate it as he had done.

I enjoyed the gift, not only because I had enjoyed our association and friendship over many years, but also because the book was a fascinating account of the way broadsheets were used to disseminate news, false news, scurrilous rumours and simple entertainment. This made me feel that a well researched book on the general subject of Street Literature would be both valuable and entertaining in the field of communications. This Street Literature was really the forerunner of the 'Popular Press' as we know it today.

Professor Collison, who has studied this material extensively, both here and in the United States, was an ideal choice of author. He readily accepted the commission to write the book and will, I know, understand my wish to dedicate the idea for it to Charles Folkard.

F. J. MARTIN DENT

Contents

Note on the Illustrations

Illustrations on pages 16, 19, 26, 32, 111, 112–13, 134, 144, 148, 149, 158–9 are reproduced from *Chap-books of the eighteenth century, with facsimiles, notes, and introduction,* by John Ashton, 1882. The others are reproduced from *The Life and Times of James Catnach (late of Seven Dials) ballad monger,* by Charles Hindley, 1878.

Foreword

Lawrence Clark Powell

This book is a significant addition to the literature on British street literature, combining history, biography, folklore, as well as samples of the lively genre. I have known and admired its author for more than twenty years. We met first in London when he was the head of the Westminster Central Reference Library. In 1951–2 he spent a year at UCLA as a member of the Library's reference staff. This led me to hope that he would join our faculty when the Graduate Library School first opened in 1960. We lost out to the British Broadcasting Corporation. In 1958 Robert L. Collison began a decade of distinguished service as Chief Librarian of that great agency. Then at last Robert Vosper and Andrew Horn succeeded in bringing Mr Collison back to UCLA as Chief Reference Librarian and Professor of Library Service. In these two major positions he has continued to enhance his reputation as a bibliographical scholar.

Whether it be as a writer, or helper of students and faculty, or teacher and administrator, Professor Collison is a virtuoso. I have always held him up to my students as the perfect bookman—learned, inquiring, energetic, imaginative, and cordial. No back-office administrator, he is to be found where the action is—on the reference desk, fielding questions with graceful authority; at the card catalog and book indices, filling gaps in the Library's holdings; in the stacks, learning by contact with books; in the classroom, dispensing knowledge with wit and charm.

Many are the instances I could give of this man's rare qualities in action. There is left only space enough to say that I hold Rob Collison in fondest esteem, and I commend this latest work to all who would be at once informed and entertained.

Malibu, California

Author's
Acknowledgments

For the opportunity to examine so many rare examples of street literature I am particularly indebted to Mr Wilbur H. Smith and his colleagues in the Department of Special Collections at the Library of the University of California, Los Angeles. Additional items of note are treasured possessions of the Bodleian Library, the Library of the American Antiquarian Society, the Library of St Bride's Institute, the City Library of Exeter, and the Central Public Library of Reading. Many more are in private collections, and many more still remain to be discovered. To those collectors who have allowed me to examine their own examples I am deeply grateful.

1 January 1972   R. C.

We have choice of Songs & merry books too,
All Pleasant and Witty, Delightful & New
Which every young Swain may whistle at Plough,
And every fair Milkmaid may sing to her Cow.
Then Maidens and Men, Come see what you lack,
And buy the fine toys that I have in my pack.

The Sorrowful Lamentation of the Pedlars, and Petty
Chapmen, for the hardness of the times, and the decay of trade,
c. 1750

If he be a seller of Books, he is no meere Bookseller one who selleth merely ynck and paper bundled up together for his owne advantage only; but he is the Chapman of Arts, of wisdom, and of much experience.

GEORGE WITHER, 1632

Introduction

Charles the footman, in the early days of his servitude, met a pedlar from whom he bought for a penny 'a little book, containing a story of a woman at Devizes, who was struck dead on the spot for telling a lie'. This Heavenly intervention saved him from the same sin, as he points out in the little chapbook that recounted his story of a blameless life. The fact was that in the first part of the nineteenth century, the penny chapbooks and the penny broadsides were always at hand in the city streets, where they fluttered on the walls to tempt passers-by. And to Charles, as he ruminated on what explanation he could give for accidentally breaking a bottle of wine which he had been carrying to one of his master's parishioners, it was natural enough that he should join the idlers who looked over the chapman's wares. Not everyone was a buyer, but there was sufficient trade to keep the chapman alive and the printers in business in marketing the ballads, the traditional tales, the account of the latest murder, and the patriotic songs that were always in such demand.

The purchasers were of all kinds. In Mrs Braddon's novel *Lady Lisle*, there is an interesting picture of Betty Jane, the scullery maid who 'leaned her head against the brass rim of the high fender, and composed herself to the perusal of an interesting fiction in penny numbers, entitled *Rodolf with the Red Hand*'. And the housebreaker, in Elizabeth Grey's *Good Society*, whiled away the time until the owner of the house departed by taking 'a badly printed kind of newspaper periodical out of his pocket, which was illustrated with wood engravings of rather a startling character, unfolded it, and commenced reading the tale of:

The Maniac Mother
or
Love and Blood

by Lady Selina de Courtenay'

As George Meredith pointed out in *Rhoda Fleming*: 'You can buy any amount for a penny, now-a-days—poetry up in a corner, stories, tales o' temptation.'

The supply of chapbooks and broadsheets and songs was widespread in the countryside too. No fair or market day was complete without the display of the latest offerings from the printers in the larger towns nearby. And the pedlars who made frequent visits to the more isolated farmhouses and cottages could be relied upon to include, among the ribbons and threads and trinkets they carried, a selection of penny readings of which at least some would be tales of giants and witches to tempt the children.

A penny in those days was not inconsiderable and not lightly squandered. But the chapbooks were, in spite of their bad type, crude illustrations, and frequent misspellings, good value for they filled their twenty-four pages, so that the youngster looking for space on which to scribble found little encouragement in the narrow margins and the lack of blank pages. For a penny was offered a text which was rarely below 5,500 words and sometimes reached almost 7,000. If the main story was too short, the remaining space would be filled with a short story, or with one or two anecdotes. Since the booklet would be thumbed to pieces by everyone who could read, the price was certainly not too high.

The broadsheets were single sheets of coarse paper, printed on one side only. Many of them reproduced ballads, humorous verse, patriotic songs, election propaganda, satires on the government or the royal family or the local town council—but a large number of them were devoted to accounts of the latest crime. If it was a murder, then there was almost inevitably the condemned man's dying confession, a letter to his mother, or a verse account of his crime which skated over the details given in small print in the lengthy report of the trial. The coarse paper and the printing on only one side of the page give the clue: they were intended for pasting on walls, and so they were, on the walls of alehouses as well as those of cottages and farm kitchens. There is always the chance that even now broadsheets long vanished may still be discovered under the layers of wallpaper—as many as twenty layers have been found in some cottages—of some remote farmhouse.

The production of chapbooks and broadsheets was no small matter. The winning of a battle, the birth of a prince, or the committing of some dreadful crime was occasion for the manufacture of thousands of broadsheets. The reprinting of the well-established contents of chapbooks went on endlessly, and a great army of people was engaged in producing and selling them. The printer was often the publisher as well, and he usually sold much of his wares direct to the pedlars. Some of the pedlars were just chapmen, whose trade in penny publications was but one part of an enterprise that embraced so much more in the way of fairings and gewgaws that could be much more profitable. A discount of only one-third meant that the sale of a chapbook was money hardly earned. But there was another type of salesman, the patterer, who operated in a different fashion.

The patterer did not limit himself to the display of his broadsheets—he declaimed them to crowds, he sang the jingles, and he poured forth the more alarming details of the murders and robberies that were then before the courts. By this means, many copies could be sold at once at the market-place, or on the corner of a city street, or in a crowded alehouse. The patterers were the popular minstrels of the eighteenth century and much of the first part of the nineteenth. Some of the best, such as Dougal Graham of Glasgow, were nationally famous—but most of them had only a local reputation.

The authorship of both broadsheets and chapbooks is largely anonymous and the writers will never be known. Many of them were versifiers of little talent who earned an uncertain livelihood by carrying out urgent commissions from the printers who wanted a dying speech or a rhyming confession in time for next morning's execution. At a pinch, a printer such as Catnach could rap out a jingle himself, and Thomas Gent, of York, could achieve something much more considerable. Of all that has survived, there are no masterpieces and no works of true literary merit, but there are many flashes of a natural instinct for the apt phrase that rescue the whole from mere drivel.

The one connecting thread running through the whole history of chapbooks and broadsheets is the large number of their printers. Looking at what is known of their generally obscure background, it is at first difficult to descry anything in common beyond the fact that none of them was a printer of the first rank. As journeymen printers they had all grown up to know that there was a ready and almost constant market for very cheap publications that could easily be defined from the experience of their predecessors. The buyers of their products were uncritical of type and layout, spelling or paper, and they cared little if the rough woodcuts had small relevance to the text. On the other hand, they had clear ideas about their likes and dislikes: the traditional stories of Jack the Giant-killer and Puss-in-Boots must not vary from the incidents that everyone knew by heart. The accounts of crimes must follow what was known about them; if the criminal was reprieved, then the lively details of his execution would be rejected by the reader.

Thus all the successful producers of this form of literature were men who kept in touch with the popular fancy, who had an instinct for what political satires would be welcome, and what—considering the power of the law—were best avoided. And to be successful they need not be too squeamish about copying word for word, and illustration for illustration, the more salable publications of their rivals. Moreover they had to be energetic enough to work all night to meet a sudden demand, or to beat their competitors at getting their wares on the street first. It was a tough but rewarding world, where there was no room for the lackadaisical.

James Catnach certainly met all these requirements and many more. Catnach was born at Alnwick in Northumberland in 1792, the son of a Scottish printer. His father produced a number of well-printed works, mostly volumes of poetry, illustrated by artists such as Thomas and John Bewick and Luke Clennell. When the Catnach family removed to Newcastle-upon-Tyne they fell on evil days, the firm was bankrupt, and they removed again, this time to London. Here too they fared badly, and at the age of twenty-one Catnach found himself in charge of his mother and sisters. With only the aid of one of his father's old wooden presses and an assortment of types and woodcuts, Catnach set himself to produce the kinds of chapbooks and broadsides which had long been in vogue in the North. His home and printing shop were one and the same building, situated in the historic and unsalubrious Monmouth Court, Seven Dials. He was the newest of several printers of this kind, and therefore faced serious opposition, but his industry and his flair for producing items that would sell rapidly gradually earned him a lasting success.

Catnach almost cornered the market in a wide range of publications for children that sold at a halfpenny or even a farthing and, as he was not over-particular concerning type or the choice of relevant illustrations, he was able to print rapidly and at small cost. He was also adept in putting out broadsides at the right moment on any crime or scandal that occupied the public's attention, as well as historic occasions such as a battle or a royal event. In addition, there was a steady income to be gained from printing tradesmen's cards, posters, theatre programmes and other fugitive items; and there was a very brisk trade every Christmas in the sale of carols.

When Catnach was twenty-seven he overreached himself and found himself in prison. His crime had been to print a libel about a local butcher called Thomas Pizzey which included the following:

Another dreadful discovery! Being an account of a number of Human Bodies found in the shop of a Pork Butcher. We have just been informed of a most dreadful and horrible discovery revolting to every feeling of humanity and calculated to inspire sentiments of horror and disgust in the minds of every Individual. On Saturday night last the Wife of a Journeyman Taylor went into the Shop of a Butcher in the neighbourhood of D[rury] L[ane] to buy a piece of Pork. At the time the Master was serving a man came into the Shop carrying a Sack. The woman thought by the appearance of the man that he was a Body Snatcher and when she left the Shop she communicated her suspicions to an acquaintance she met with; the news of this soon spread abroad and two Officers went and searched the house and to their inexpressible horror found two dead bodies wrapped up in a sack great flocks of people were assembled from all parts of the Town at Marlborough Street in expectation of the offender having a hearing.

As a result of the rumour and Catnach's flier about 200 people went to Pizzey's shop, broke in and knocked him and his family about and did a certain amount of damage. Pitts, Catnach's rival, added to his discomfort by issuing lampoons such as this one:

Jemmy Catnach printed a quarter sheet—
    It was called in lanes and passages,
That Pizzey the butcher had dead bodies chopped,
    And made them into sausages.

Poor Pizzey was in an awful mess,
    And looked the colour of cinders—
A crowd assembled from far and near,
    And they smashed in all his windows.

Now Jemmy Catnach's gone to prison,
    And what's he gone to prison for?
For printing a libel against Mr. Pizzey,
    Which was sung from door to door.

Six months in quad old Jemmy got,
    Because he a shocking tale had started,
About Mr. Pizzey who dealt in sausages
    In Blackmore Street, Clare Market.

Catnach's family carried on the business, while he served out his term at the Clerkenwell House of Correction, but they too ran foul of the law in a minor way and his mother was severely reprimanded by the Bow Street magistrate for publishing a halfpenny broadsheet with details of a fictitious murder. The Catnachs were, however, a tough and resilient family and once 'Jemmy' was released they got down to the work of rebuilding their fortunes. There was plenty to win by acting expeditiously: Catnach made £500 by his penny accounts of John Thurtell's sensational murder of William Weare in 1832—which meant that he must have sold about a quarter of a million copies of his own production, in the face of keen opposition from his rivals! The total sale for the last dying speech and confession of any outstanding criminal could reach sales of well in excess of a million in those days.

Catnach died a bachelor in 1841. During his meteoric career in London he had lived through a vast number of stirring events—Queen Caroline's disgrace and trial, the accession of Queen Victoria and her marriage to Prince Albert, the introduction of the railways and the setting up of the police force, the struggles of the Chartists, the troubles that accompanied the Reform Bill—and the committing of a very wide and sensational series of crimes. He never failed to take advantage of any of these, and by doing so he created from nothing a printing and publishing house which, although it was never very large—employing only four or five staff—was responsible for the issue of several million copies of the most fugitive (but the most read) of all literature.

Catnach's greatest rival, John Pitts, was born, the son of a baker, at Effingham in Norfolk in 1765. He may have got some training as a printer prior to his arrival in London and, after further experience in the Metropolis, he eventually set up his own business in Great St Andrew Street, Seven Dials, in 1802. Pitts made a particular hit in the publication of halfpenny ballads, many of which came from a much earlier period. His first serious opposition came from the upstart Catnach. The Grub Street writers who produced the new topical ballads, the bogus 'dying confessions' of criminals, and the political squibs of the day, were of course supposed to be loyal to one or other of the rival houses, and if they were discovered to be trading with 'the enemy' they could expect no mercy. The rivalry was purely commercial: there was in fact trade enough to make both Pitts and Catnach rich. They were not of course without other rivals—there were at least eight in the immediate vicinity of Seven Dials, and more in other parts of London. Pitts survived Catnach, dying in 1844, but the younger man had proved the more successful. Nevertheless Pitts's achievement had been substantial, and noticeably he had a much better taste in his woodcuts, employing more talented artists to produce illustrations with some relevance to the texts they decorated. His sense of typographical layout was superior to

Catnach's, and some of his title pages have a balance and elegance which his rival never managed to achieve.

Better production was in fact often to be found in the provinces and abroad. James Kendrew of York, John Cheney and J. G. Rusher of Banbury and Isaiah Thomas of Worcester, Massachusetts, all printed finer works than most of the items that were issued in London. On the other hand the productions of the printers in Glasgow and Newcastle-upon-Tyne were often shoddy and, in some places, unreadable.

Nevertheless Pitts, Catnach and many of their rivals appear from the little that is known of them to have been rough, tough and uncouth opportunists. In contrast their famous predecessor, Dougal Graham, the 'Skellat Bellman' of Glasgow, is very much more attractive as a personality. Motherwell, the poet, called him 'the Scottish Rabelais' and 'the Vulgar Juvenal of the age'. Graham was 'a curious, little witty fellow, with a round face and a broad nose'. He was born at Raploch, near Stirling, about 1724, and suffered from indifferent health throughout his life. Nevertheless he was very active and, during the Forty-Five, he accompanied the Pretender's army throughout its unhappy campaign, and in 1746 published a poetical account of the rebellion in Hudibrastic metre amounting to over 5,000 lines. This was instantly successful and ran through twenty editions by 1828. After the war he made a living as a chapman, travelling through the counties of Stirling, Lanark, the Lothians, Dumbarton and Fife. But he was not only a chapman; he wrote many of the chapbooks and poems and songs he sold, and soon the booksellers of Glasgow, Paisley, Stirling and Falkirk were competing for his publications.

Their success enabled him to set up his own printing office in the Saltmarket at Glasgow. This was not his only piece of good fortune. About 1772 he applied for the important post of 'Skellat Bellman'—that is, Bellman to the city of Glasgow. That year there was unusually

numerous competition for the honour, and a public trial of the candidates'
skill was arranged. Graham, suspect as a Jacobite, was not to the taste of
the Hanoverian city magistrates, but his popularity as a poet and a wit
counted in his favour with the ordinary citizens:

> The trial of skill took place in the court behind the old Town's Hospital,
> near the Clyde; and the popular traditional account of the event represents
> Dougal as the hero of the occasion. After the other candidates had tried
> the strength of their lungs and the reach of their voices on the announce-
> ment of 'Fresh herrings at the Broomielaw', he sang at the top of his
> voice, with simulated gravity, in a manner that put them all in the shade:
> > 'Caller herring at the Broomielaw,
> > Three a penny, three a penny.'
>
> But remembering that it was not the season for fresh herring, he added,
> with the comic confidence for which he was distinguished—
> > 'But indeed, my friends, it is a' a blawflum,
> > For the herring's no catch'd and the boat's no come.'
>
> Dougal was elected unanimously, and the traditional fame of his bell-
> manship leaves no doubt that he discharged the duties of the office to the
> satisfaction of the magistrates and the advantage and entertainment of
> the public.

The post of City bellman was more important than it would seem today.
The Bellman attended the meetings of the city council dressed in the
traditional livery of the office. There was an annual salary of £10, and
much more could be added since the local merchants used the bellman
as their chief advertising medium. But there was plenty of time left for
Graham to conduct his own business and to continue his writing.
Graham persevered in the revision of his poem on the Rebellion, issuing
a third edition in 1774. But by 1779 Graham was dead and was com-
memorated in an anonymous poem:

> Ye mothers fond! Oh! be not *blate*
> To mourn poor Dougal's hapless fate;
> Oft times, you know, he did you get
> > Your wandered *weans*;
> To find them out both *air* and late
> > He spared no pains.
>
> Of witty jokes he had such store,
> Johnson could not have pleased you more;
> Or, with Loud laughter, made you roar
> > As he could do;
> He still had something ne'er before
> > Exposed to view.

8

The function that the chapbook, and more especially the broadsheet, played as a substitute for the newspaper throughout the eighteenth century and part of the nineteenth stems from a number of causes. This aspect is truer of the provinces than of the Metropolis, but throughout Britain they were the forerunners of the popular newspapers from 1712 onwards. Initially the penny duty per sheet was introduced in that year * as a means of raising additional revenue. But in 1776 the duty had increased to 1½d. and in 1789 to 2d. By 1797 it was 3½d. and from 1815 onwards it had risen to 4d. It was not reduced to 1d. until 1836 and only finally abolished in 1855. The resulting high prices of newspapers put them beyond the range of most working people, though there were expedients in sharing (and even renting) newspapers that enabled the most zealous town readers to keep in regular touch with the events of the day. The supply was, however, small for most of the period—it has been estimated that in the year 1790, for example, only one copy of a newspaper was available for every 300 inhabitants. The position worsened later: in 1817 one innkeeper said that two daily newspapers cost him twenty pounds annually.

Another significant factor was the poor distribution of newspapers: the nearest supplies might be no closer than the nearest market town, so that rural workers, even if they shared the expense, found it difficult to get a regular supply. The introduction of the full resources of the paper-making machine—patented in England in 1801—was delayed through trade opposition for nearly twenty years; and cylinder printing by steam power, discovered by William Nicholson in 1790, was not used in England until 1814. Thus the cheaper methods of publication, which offered such advances in speed and numbers of copies printed, coincided with the highest rating duty on newspapers.

An additional factor that is hard to assess is the degree of literacy of working people in the eighteenth and early nineteenth centuries. Burke estimated that there were 80,000 readers in England in the 1790s, but he was presumably referring only to people able to read widely. It is clear that with all the efforts of the evangelical charity schools and the Methodist Sunday schools, dating from the last half of the eighteenth century, there was a very much larger number of people who had some reading knowledge. On the other hand the many references to reading aloud from newspapers in inns and coffee-houses show that the sustained reading of literary English was beyond the ability of a large proportion of the population, and that in many instances, they were willing to pay for this service.

---

* Separate duties were levied on paper, on newspapers and pamphlets, and on advertisements. By 1815 pamphlets of one sheet were no longer stamped.

With so many difficulties to contend with, the workers, and even more their families, had only infrequent access to newspapers. Moreover there were no popular newspapers written at a level to suit their background and interests. The chapbooks and the broadsides therefore filled a gap. While they might have heard of a criminal's being brought to trial, they might hear little of the outcome, until the broadside arrived with the whole of the story. This applied to historical events as well—the details of a naval victory, a royal event or a political squabble must wait on the arrival of the broadside, which not only reprinted the details in the press but relayed it in ballad form as well. The latter point was especially important: illiterate people often have remarkable memories—aided by the recommended and familiar tune at the head of the ballad, many a listener would effortlessly commit the verses to memory after hearing them only two or three times. The language was simple, the rhymes crude but memorable. To a large mass of the population the chapbooks and the broadsides filled a need that was not otherwise met until the introduction of the popular press in the 1850s.

1. Traditional

The school mistress in *Our Mutual Friend*, when writing an essay, could always fill a slate, starting at the top left hand corner and finishing in the bottom right hand corner. Chapbooks were equally economical of space. Almost invariably they comprised twenty-four pages, which meant they could be constructed of one sheet of paper about 16 inches by 18 inches which, printed on both sides folded ingeniously twice one way and then twice the other, yielded the required amount of pages; the order of the pages had to be carefully planned in advance (see page 12).

Sometimes an error would result in one or more of the pages being printed out of order. Little care was taken over the folding or trimming of the pages, so that occasionally the last line or so of a crowded page would carelessly be shaved off. Badly inked type, crooked lines, and a general policy of 'anything goes' meant that the buyer sometimes felt baffled as he tried to make out the words or sense of what he was trying to read. There were no covers to the chapbooks, the front of the first page serving as title-page, on which a woodcut—often the only one in the booklet—served as decoration.

These woodcuts were never pensioned off as long as they could be made to produce some kind of blurred picture. Their choice moreover was often haphazard. A Turk with baggy trousers and a great curved sword decorates the title-page of a life of Dick Turpin, and reappears on *The Irish Assassin*. St George and the Dragon are depicted on the life of the gentleman-robber Redmond O'Hanlon. The royal arms appear on *The Golden Dreamer*, a dream interpreter. A Roman centurion does duty on a tale of medieval Italy, the story of Hero and Leander, and

FRONT   BACK

10	15	22	3	4	21	16	9
⅃	8Ɩ	6Ɩ	9	⑆	0ᄅ	⅄Ɩ	8
12	13	24	1	2	23	14	11

Note that if the pages are to come out in the right sequence and position when the sheet is folded, the middle section on both front and back of the sheet must be printed upside down.

the 'famous history of Valentine and Orson'. A handsome eighteenth-century house decorates the tale of Cinderella.

Not all the woodcuts on chapbooks were so unsuited to their contents: there is a magnificent giant—strongly contrasted with a puny Jack and a captive damsel—on the cover of Jack the Giant Killer; and on Dr Faustus there is Faust himself, robust and expectant, looking in his cocked hat very much like a magnificent toby jug. A charming scene in idyllic surroundings decorates *The Village Curate*. The life of Mahomet is, however, the most surprising, for he is depicted in the costume, and looking every inch the part, of an eighteenth-century divine (the same block appearing on the life of the Rev. John Welch (1570–1623) seems to have been a little more appropriately placed!). There were of course some exceptions: some chapbooks were not decorated at all, and there were also some which were only twelve pages long, while others were as much as thirty-six.

Sometimes the back of the title-page was left blank but, if there was enough text, the story began there. Occasionally it was used as an advertisement listing other books in the same series, as in this example from the Newcastle-upon-Tyne publisher Bowman, of 12 Nun's Lane:

Penny Histories

Crown 12mo. Three or upwards sent post free to any address, on receipt of stamps to the amount.

1. The Golden Dreamer
2. Mother Bunch's Fortune Teller
3. Napoleon's Book of Fate
4. Watty and Meg
5. The Dreamer's Oracle
6. Jane Shore
7. The Generous Man
8. Dick Turpin, the Highwayman
9. Mary the Maid of the Inn
10. Shepherdess of the Alps and Count Fonroso
11. A Voyage in the Coal Trade
12. The Hermit of Warkworth
13. The Life of George Buchanan
14. The Life of the Earl of Derwentwater
15. The Long Pack, a Northumbrian Tale
16. The Maid and the Magpie
17. Robinson Crusoe
18. George Barnwell
19. The Lambton Worm, and the Cowed Lad of Hilton
20. The New Guide to Matrimony
21. The Life of Jack Shepherd
22. The Battle of Chevy Chase
23. Shamus O'Brien, the Bould Boy of Glingall

The selection was of course vast, for there were so many printers engaged in the business, and competition was keen among them. Bowman did not rely on the postal trade, freely advertising, 'Shopkeepers and Hawkers Supplied on the lowest terms'. All the printers gave discounts so that their chapbooks could continue to be sold at a penny each, and some of the booksellers invited their customers to choose one or two more free of charge, if they had bought several already.

The steadiest sellers over the years comprised a comparatively small number of well-known tales. Jack Sheppard, 'the notorious house and gaol breaker', could always find readers, for the account of his jail-breaks was so extraordinary that the public were fascinated by them:

Sheppard was now a second time in the hands of justice; but Jack knew his trade too well to remain long in such a thraldom. He and his mate were now in a strong and well guarded prison [New Prison, in London], himself loaded with a pair of double links and basils, of about 14 lbs. weight, and confined together in the safe apartment, called Newgate Ward. Sheppard, conscious of his crimes, and knowing the information he had made to be but a blind scheme that would avail him nothing, began to meditate an escape. They had been thus detained four days, and their friends having the liberty of seeing them, furnished him with implements proper for his design. Accordingly Sheppard went to work, and on the 25th May [1724], being Whitsunday, at about two o'clock in the morning, completed a practicable breach, and sawed off his fetters; having, with unheard-of diligence and dexterity cut off an iron bar from the window, and took out a mutin or bar, of the most solid oak, about nine inches in thickness, by boring it through in many places with great skill and labour. They had still twenty-five feet to descend. Sheppard fastened a sheet and blankets to the bars, caused madam to take off her gown and petticoat, and sent her out first. She being more corpulent than himself, it was with much difficulty he got her through the opening, but, on observing his directions, she was instantly down more frightened than hurt. Our hero followed, and alighted with ease and pleasure. But where are they escaped to? Why, out of the prison into another. The reader is to understand that the New Prison and Clerkenwell Bridewell lie contiguous to each other, and they had got into the yard of the latter, and had a wall of twenty-two feet high to scale before their liberty was perfected. Sheppard, far from being unprepared to surmount this difficulty, had his gimlet and pincers ready, and made a scaling ladder. While the keepers and prisoners of both places were asleep in their beds, he mounts with his lady, and in less than ten minutes carries both her and himself over the wall, and completes an entire escape. Although his escape from the condemned hole in Newgate made a far greater noise in the world than that from the New Prison, it has been allowed by all the gaol-keepers in London, that one so extra-ordinary was never performed in England before. The broken chairs and bars are kept in the New Prison to testify and preserve the memory of this act.

THE TRIAL, SENTENCE, FULL CONFESSION, AND EXECUTION OF
BISHOP & WILLIAMS,
THE BURKERS.

As the latter escape was just as spectacular, it is no wonder that thousands of copies of this closely and ill-printed chapbook were sold for much more than a century.

The life of Paul Jones, the pirate, was told in a much less dramatic style, but as the events themselves were well within the memory of many people still living, and as it was supported by the full text of the official report of Captain Pearson to the Lords of the Admiralty concerning the disastrous naval action off Scarborough, there was plenty for anyone interested in the stirring events of the American War of Independence. The life of Dick Turpin, as told in the chapbooks, was by no means as romantic as present-day accounts. Black Bess, his famous mount, plays a very small part, and the renowned ride to York is made little of. Most of Turpin's raids are described, as they in fact were, as cowardly acts of violence against an ill-policed and largely helpless citizenry. Nevertheless, without depicting him as other than an unscrupulous villain, the writers did justice to his few acts of compassion:

> Another time he robbed a poor woman returning from Ferrybridge, where she had been to sell some commodities; and soon after hearing she was distressed by her landlord for rent, he contrived to relieve her in the following singular manner. He found out her abode, and threw into the window, through the glass, a leather bag containing gold and silver to the amount of six pounds; perhaps the produce of a recent robbery.

At the end of the story there is a whiff of Burke and Hare activities when the mob, who had witnessed his execution, found that his body had been stolen. Suspecting it was to be anatomized, they tracked it down, rescued it, carried it away in triumph, and reburied it, having first filled the coffin with slacked lime.

Robin Hood's adventures were so rooted in a folk memory of four centuries that they warranted recounting in verse:

> Both gentlemen and yeomen bold,
> or whatever you are;
> To hear a stately story told,
> attention now prepare:

and the tale goes on to tell how the much admired Earl of Huntington lived and entertained too well, until his fortune was consumed and he was outlawed by the Crown. The poem goes on to give rather a different picture of the outlawed 'Robin Hood' from today's version:

His chiefest spite to the clergy was,
    that liv'd in monstrous pride;
No one of them he could let pass
    along the highway side;
But first they must to dinner go,
    and afterwards to shrift;
Full many a one he served so,
    thus while he liv'd by theft.

No monks or friars he would let go,
    without paying their fees;
If they thought much to be used so,
    their gear he made them leave.
For such as they the country fill'd
    with bastards in those days;
Which to prevent those sparks did geld
    all that came in their ways.

But Robin Hood so gently was,
    and bore so brave a mind,
If any in distress should pass,
    to them he was so kind,
That he would give and lend to them,
    to help them in their need;
Thus made all poor men pray for him
    and wish he well might speed.

16

Unlike the modern anecdotes of Robin Hood's struggles with the Sheriff of Nottingham, the poem makes no mention of this, but concentrates on his feud with the clergy, particularly the Abbot of St Mary's to whom he owed money, and later with the powerful Bishop of Ely, who was both Chancellor and Viceroy during Richard Cœur de Lion's absence overseas. On the return of the King, Robin Hood makes overtures which are well received, but his motley band of outlaws melts away in fear that the King's vengeance will reach them. At last, Robin Hood finding himself alone, falls into a fever and retreats to a nunnery where he is bled to death by a perfidious friar. At the end of the poem there is a singular passage of moralizing:

> We that live in those latter days
>   of civil government,
> (If need be) have an hundred ways
>   such out-laws to prevent.
> In those days men more barbarous were,
>   and lived less in awe;
> Now, God be thanked, people fear,
>   more to offend the law.

and, after several further verses pursuing this theme, and warning readers to take no heed of the many legends that were current about Robin Hood, the epitaph which the Prioress of the Monastery of Kirkslay in Yorkshire set over his grave, is given:

> Decembris quarto Die 1198. Anno Regis
> Richardi, Primi IX.
> Robert, Earl of Huntington,
> Lies under this little stone;
> No archer was like him so good,
> His wildness nam'd him Robin Hood,
> Full thirteen years and something more,
> These northern parts he vexed sore
> Such out-laws as he and his men
> May England never know again.

When Dr Faustus stabbed his wrist to write his agreement with the Devil, his blood cooled so fast in the little saucer as if it forewarned him of the hellish act he was going to commit. Nevertheless he put it over embers to warm it, and wrote as follows:

I, John Faustus, approved doctor of divinity, with my own hand do acknowledge and testify myself to become a servant to Lucifer, Prince of Septentrional and Oriental, and to him I freely and voluntarily give both body and soul; in consideration for the space of twenty four years, if I be served in all things which I shall require, or which is reasonable by him to be allowed; at the expiration of which time from the date ensuing, I give to him all power to do with me at his pleasure; to rule to fetch and carry me where he pleases body and soul; hereupon I defy God and Christ, and the host of angels and good spirits all living creatures that bear his shape, or on whom his image is imprinted; and to the better strengthening of this covenant and firm agreement between us, I have writ it with my blood, and subscribe my name to it, calling all the powers and infernal potentates to witness it is my true intent and meaning.

JOHN FAUSTUS.

This somewhat incoherent document had the unique effect of offering the reader two separate delights. In the first place, what would Faust do with his newly acquired powers? And, since the reader already knew that it was Faust's secret intention to outwit the Devil, what would happen at midnight on the 365th day of the 24th year after this agreement was signed? The answers are somewhat surprising: far from making much personal use of his pact with the Devil, Faust divided his time between playing a number of crude practical tricks, and doing two or three good turns, such as helping a young man to a wife who had formerly spurned him. When the twenty-four years were almost up, Faust began to grow fearful and even to repent momentarily, but there was no escape and he was torn to shreds by the Devil and his soul cast into Hell—a place of which he had had a glimpse many years before:

he saw hell divided into several cells, or deep holes; and for every cell, or deep ward, there was a devil appointed to punish those that were under his custody. Having seen this sight he much marvelled at it; and at that time Mephistophiles being with him, he asked him what sort of people they were that lay in the first dark pit; then Mephistophiles told him they were those who pretended themselves to be physicians, and who had poisoned many thousands to try practise; and now saith the spirit they have just the same administered to them, which they gave to others though not with the same effect, for they will never die here saith he. Over their heads was a shelf laden with gallipots full of poison. Having past them he came to a long entry exceeding dark where there was a mighty crowd, he asked them what those were? and the spirit told him they were pickpockets; who loved to be in a crowd, when they were in the other world, and to content them they put them in a crowd there, amongst them were some padders on the high way, and those of that function. Walking farther he saw many thousands of vintners, and some millions of taylors, in so much that they could not feel where to get stowage for them; a great number of pastry cooks with peels on their heads. Walking farther, the spirit opening a great cellar door, from which arose a terrible noise, he asked what they were; the spirit told him they were witches, and those who had been pretended Saints in the other world; but how they did squabble, fight, and tear one another. Not far from them lay the whore mongers and adulterers, who made such a hideous noise; that he was very much startled. Walking down a few steps he espied an incredible number almost hid with smoke; he asked what they were? the spirit told him they were millers and bakers; but good lack, what a noise there was among them! The millers crying to the bakers, and the bakers crying to the millers for help, but all was in vain, for there was none to help them. Passing on still farther, he saw thousands of shopkeepers, some of whom he knew, who were tormented for defrauding and cheating their customers.

Valentine and Orson, a tale now forgotten, had a tremendous vogue in the days of the chapbook, and was also enacted on the London stage. The two brothers had been separated by accident at birth, Orson being brought up by a bear, and Valentine as a noble in the court of King Pepin. Valentine, hearing of the depredations of the wild and speechless Orson, set out to capture him and brought him back to court, where he set about the work of civilizing him. Later they both went to Aquitaine where they set about the task of defeating the Green Knight, a pagan champion, whom no one had been able to withstand. Orson overcame him, and the Green Knight agreed to turn Christian and to enter the King's service. Valentine and Orson then sailed away to a tower of burnished brass where they consulted the oracle of an enchanted head of brass standing between four pillars of pure jasper. Here they at last learnt that they were brothers, and the long-lost sons of the Emperor of Greece. Orson's speech was restored by cutting a thread beneath his tongue.

The brother of Valentine's wife, Clerimond, was a giant called Ferragus, a Mohammedan living in Portugal. The reduction of this monster is followed by the attack of Brandiffer—brother of Ferragus—on the city of Constantinople. The Mohammedan was defeated, but in the fierce battle Valentine killed his own father by accident. Greatly troubled by his misfortune, Valentine travelled to the East, made pilgrimage to the Holy Sepulchre and eventually died. Orson, later turned hermit, returned to the woods of his childhood where he stayed until his death many years later. Throughout this very detailed story, the emergence of the reign of Charlemagne and the incessant wars of Europe with the Islamic forces are as prominent as the tale of the two brothers, and in spite of the magical nature of the story, there is a strong undercurrent of the stormy unrest which faced the government of France of those times.

The theme of the two young men who face life's dangers together, and eventually suffer disaster reappears in the tragedy of Bewick and Graham, sons of the rival knights. As a result of idle drunken boasting between the two fathers, the two boys are made to fight each other.

> When Graham did see his bully* come,
>   The salt tears stood long in his e'e,
> Now needs must I say, thou art a man,
>   That dare venture thy body to fight with me.
>
> Nay, I have a harness on my back,
>   I know that thou hast none on thine:
> But as little as thou hast on thy back,
>   As little shall there be on mine.
>
> He flang his jacket from off his back,
>   His cap of steel from his head flang he,
> He's taken his spear into his hand,
>   He's ty'd his horse unto a tree.
>
> Now they fell to it with two broad swords,
>   For two long hours fought Bewick and he,
> Much sweat was to be seen on them both,
>   But never a drop of blood to see.
>
> Now Graham gave Bewick an awkward stroke,
>   An awkward stroke surely struck he,
> He struck him under the left breast,
>   Then down to the ground as dead fell he.
>
> Arise, arise, O bully Bewick,
>   Arise, and speak three words to me.
> Is this to be thy deadly wound,
>   Or God and good surgeons will mend thee?

* friend.

O horse, O horse, O bully Graham,
    And pray do get thee far from me,
Thy sword it is sharp, it hath wounded my heart,
    And so no farther can I gae.

O horse, O horse, O bully Graham,
    And get thee far from me with speed,
And get thee out of this country quite,
    That not one may know who's done the deed.

Oh! if this be true, my bully dear,
    The words that thou dost tell to me,
The vow I made, and the vow I'll keep,
    I swear I'll be the first to die.

Then he stuck his sword in a nould-hill,
    And he leapt thirty good feet and three,
First he bequeath'd his soul to God,
    And upon his own sword leapt he.

Now Graham he was the first that died;
    And then Sir Robert Bewick came to see;
Arise, arise, O son, he said
    For I see thou's won the victory.

Father, could not you drink your wine at home,
    And letten me and my bully be,
Now dig a grave both low and wide,
    And in it us two pray bury?
But bury my bully Graham on the sun side,
    For I'm sure he's won the victory.

This emphasis on the inestimable value of constancy to the death occurs
in different forms in many chapbook stories, of which the outstanding
must be *The Famous History of Two Unfortunate Lovers, Hero and Leander*.
Leander's wooing of Hero, beset as it was with fresh obstacles in every
chapter, is given a continuity all of its own by the constant recurrence of
hints of impending doom by drowning. This, to readers who were

already familiar with the outcome, afforded the liveliest satisfaction, particularly the last, the Mermaids' warning:

> Awake, Leander, see the skies
> Do in the blackest tempest rise;
> In Neptune's watery kingdom
> Two lovers shall entombed be;
> Whose sad mishap the sea-gods all,
> With us lament their funeral:
> The cruel ghosts' revenge to crave,
> But fate decrees them to their grave.
>
> We pity lovers that are crost,
> And in their highest hopes so lost;
> When nearest to their hopes they seem,
> They find all but a golden dream;
> Then do cross winds bear away
> Their hopes. Leander, prithee stay;
> But thee too forward fate drives on,
> By love the best of lovers are undone.

2. Jests

Care to our coffin adds a nail no doubt,
While every laugh so merry draws one out.

The blank space in a chapbook, left at the end of a story, was filled with any matter that met the desired length. Sometimes, if there were two or three pages left, there would be a short story, but if there was less the 'filler' would be an anecdote or a joke. Little heed was given to the relevance of such matter to the principal contents: a factual account of the Black Hole of Calcutta was appended to the life of Paul Jones; a lively character sketch of Big Jack Joyce of Connemara followed the autobiography of Charles Jones the footman. The 'Tragical History of Jane Arnold, commonly called Crazy Jane' was short enough to allow for no less than seven anecdotes, of which the following is typical:

Jonathan's Hunting Excursion

'Did you ever hear of the scrape that I and Uncle Zekiel had duckin' on't on the Connecticut?' asked Jonathan Timbertoes, while amusing his old Dutch hostess who had agreed to entertain him under the roof of her log cottage, for, and in consideration of, a bran new milk pan.

'No, I never did—do tell it', was the reply.

'Well,—you must know that I and Uncle Zeke took it into our heads on Saturday afternoon to go a-gunning arter ducks in father's skiff; so in we got and skulled down river; a proper sight of ducks flew backwards and forwards, I tell you—and bimeby a few of 'em lit down by the marsh, and went to feeding on muscles. I catched up my peauder horn to prime, and it slipped right out of my hand, and sunk to the bottom of the river. The water was amazingly clear, and I could see it on the bottom. Now I couldn't swim a jot, so I sez to Uncle Zeke—"You're a pretty clever fellow—jest let me take your peauder horn to prime," and don't you think the stingy critter wouldn't. "Well," says I, "you're a pretty good diver, an' if you dive an' get it, I'll give you a primin." I thought he'd leave his peauder horn, but he didn't; but stuck it in his pocket, and down he went—and there he staid.'

Here the old lady opened her eyes with wonder and surprise, and a pause of some minutes ensued, and Jonathan added—

'I looked down, and what do you think the critter was doin'?'

'Lord!' exclaimed the old lady, 'I'm sure I don't know.'

'There he was,' said our hero, 'settin' right on the bottom of the river, pourin' the peauder out of my horn into hizen.'

CRAZY JANE.

Most of the stories at the end of the chapbooks were rather shorter than this and, from the fact that many of them were set in America or in Ireland, it is possible that they may have been 'borrowed' from other publications. A number of them are tedious in their recounting, such as the tale of the bonnet-laird who had been a heavy drinker and, deciding he should join a temperance society, tried to buy a share in the Glasgow Water Company—two pages are needed for the laird to come finally to exclaim: 'Gae wa'—gae wa', sir! Eighty-five pounds for drinking water! If that's the case, I'll stick by the speerit trade yet!' Nevertheless this tale was sufficiently popular to be reprinted in several chapbooks.

Many of the anecdotes are about practical jokes of a crudity that shows the nature of the age, though the outcome of the prank of two young noblemen who steal a cart full of buttermilk barrels, relieves the rest of the story. The old man who chases them, and indignantly watches his buttermilk spill out through the streets of Edinburgh, finally catches up with the miscreants and demands their names. One of them hands him a folded paper which he says contains the required addresses. After they have gone, the old man unfolds the paper to find it is a ten-pound note. Immediately he resumes the chase, crying out, 'Will ye need ony mair milk the morn?'

A particular target was the Irishman, and thousands of copies were sold of *The Comical Sayings of Paddy from Cork, with his Coat Buttoned Behind*. Paddy, in the course of a conversation, tells how he was forced to leave Ireland because he took an old gentleman's gun. His defence in the magistrate's court was that he had got it from his father when it was a little pistol, had kept it until it had grown into a gun, and was going to keep it until it had developed into a big cannon, at which time he intended to sell it to the military!

The rest of the chapbook never achieves even this standard again. Inappropriately, in a chapbook entitled *The Scotch Haggis*, the following occurs:

A Weather-Master

An Irish pastor, when applied to by one of his flock for a shower of rain, said he should be happy to oblige him, but he had several previous applications for dry weather; and as it would be impossible for him to disoblige any of his congregation, he was under the necessity of declining to interfere.

which is somewhat better than the Irishman who one day found a light guinea and got eighteen shillings for it. Next day he was walking and saw another. 'Allelieu dear honey,' says he, 'I'll have nothing to do with you, for I lost three shillings by your brother yesterday!'

One of the oldest of the jest books, a version of which most printers included in their lists, is *The Merry Tales of the Wise Men of Gotham*, on whose title-page often appeared:

> Of merry Books this is the chief,
> 'Twill make you laugh your fill.

These were stories that had their origin in the Middle Ages and were familiar in general to the whole population. The men of Gotham represent simpletons who are bound to bungle any task that confronts them, as in the following:

On a time the men of Gotham fain would have pinned in the cuckoo that she might sing all the year; and in the midst of the town they had a hedge made round in compass, and got a cuckoo and put her in it, and said, Sing here, and thou shalt lack neither meat nor drink all the year. The cuckoo, where she found herself encompassed by the hedge, flew away. A vengeance on her, said these wise men, we did not make our hedge high enough.

This is typical of the problems faced by the men of Gotham. Separately they reacted in a similar fashion. One of them going to market with two bushels of wheat carried them on his own back, lest his horse should have too great a burden. Such tales occur in many parts of the world. In the Isle of Wight there is the proverbial tale of the farmer who cut off the head of his sheep in order to release it from a fence—and in America many people will be familiar with the exploits recounted in *The Peterkin Papers*, such as the tale where the family buys a piano that is too large to go in the door. Sending, as they always did, for The Lady from Philadelphia, they are told to put the piano on the veranda so that they can play it through the window of their parlour.

The mischief-maker and the practical joker were great favourites among the buyers of chapbooks. One of the most popular was Leper the Tailor, whose jokes were often more ferocious than pleasant. Nevertheless, his story gives some interesting insights into the lives of apprentices and journeymen tailors in those days. In his apprenticeship Leper and his master suffered from a mean and unpleasant mistress. Since she kept all the meat for herself and fed her husband and Leper on boiled cabbage and bread, Leper managed to substitute horseflesh for her nightly meal. He terrorized a neighbour and his wife by making them believe their house was falling down. He exposed his two layabed sisters to public scorn by pretending they were dead when they were only sleeping in daytime. There are many more such incidents in which he always triumphed. Probably the best of all is his struggle with the extreme churchgoers of the city:

Leper was in use to give his lads their Sunday's supper, which obliged him
to stay from the kirk in the afternoon, he having neither wife nor servant
maid; so one Sunday afternoon as he was cooking his pot, John Muckle-
cheek, and James Puff-and-blaw, two civileers, having more zeal than
knowledge, came upon him, and said—What's the matter, sir, you go not
to the kirk? Leper replied, I'm reading my book and cooking my pot,
which I think is a work of necessity. Then says the one to the other, don't
answer that graceless fellow, we'll make him appear before his betters; so
they took the kail pot, and puts a staff through the bools, and bears it to
the Clerk's chamber. Leper who was never at a loss for invention, goes to
the Principal of the College's house, no body being at home but a lass
roasting a leg of mutton; Leper says, my dear, will you go and bring me
a drink of ale, and I'll turn the spit till you come back. The lass was no
sooner gone, than he runs away with the leg of mutton, which served his
lads and him for their supper. When the Principal came home, he was
neither to haud nor to bind he was so angry; so on Monday he goes and
makes a complaint to the Lord Provost, who sends two officers for Leper,
who came immediately. My Lord asked him how he dared to take away
the Principal's mutton? Leper replied, how dared your civileers to take
away my kail pot? I'm sure there is less sin in making a pot full of kail,
than roasting a leg of mutton, law makers should not be law breakers, so
I demand justice on the civileers. The Provost asked him what justice he
would have? says he, make them carry the pot back again; and to the
Principal, a leg of mutton will not make him and full fall out; so they
were forced to carry the pot back again, and Leper caused the boys to
huzza after them to their disgrace.

A much wittier and more entertaining chapbook was devoted to the
exploits of George Buchanan, the King's fool. George was as ingenious
and resourceful as Chicot the jester, and his life makes good reading.
Banished by James I 'from English ground', he went to Scotland, put
earth in both his boots, and returning bested the King as he had so often
done before. On another occasion he boasted to the bishop that any
Scottish shepherd could win a dispute with any London bishop. When
his challenge was taken up, George posted with all haste to the Scotish
border, disguised himself as a shepherd, and met the bishop's delegation.
Driving his flock to the roadside, he chanted a Latin ballad. As the
bishop came up, he asked George the time in French. George replied in
Hebrew that it was directly about the time of day that it was the previous
day at that time. Someone else asked him in Greek where he came from.
George replied in Flemish that if his questioner knew that he would be
as wise as himself. A third man asked him where he was educated.
George replied, in Gaelic, that he had been educated herding his sheep
between the border and Lochaber. The bishop's party decided to abandon

their mission. George, of course, made certain to be back in London well before their arrival. But the best of the many entertaining tales about George Buchanan is this one:

> The French King, in order to pick a quarrel with the English Court, sent a letter desiring it to be read before the Parliament, which was as follows:
>
> 'Will I come? will I come? will I come?'
>
> This letter being read before the King and his courtiers, they all concluded that the French designed to invade England. They ordered an answer to be wrote upbraiding him with the breach of peace, and putting him in mind of the last treaty. The answer being read over before the King and his nobles, they all agreed that it should be sent off; but George smiling and shaking his head, said—
>
> 'Many men, many minds;
> Who knows what he designs?'
>
> They then asked George what he thought the French King meant by such a letter? To which he answered, 'I suppose he wants an invitation to come over and dine with you, and then return in a friendly manner; but you are going to charge him with a breach of peace before he has given any signal of offence. His letter is indeed dark and mystical, but send him an answer according to his question.' George being asked to write the answer, wrote as follows:
>
> 'And ye come! and ye come, and ye come!'
>
> This being sent to the French King, he admired it beyond expression; saying, it was more valliant and daring than he expected. So the enmity he intended was extinguished and turned into love.

George Buchanan (1506–1582) really existed. He was a Scottish humanist and reformer and was a tutor to the young King James VI of Scotland. Though he had an exciting enough life, he was never the English King's fool. In the chapbook he is made, at the end of his life, to send the King the following reply to the message in which he demanded George's return to Court within twenty days:

> My honour'd liege, and sovereign king,
> Of your beseeching great I dread nothing,
> On your head and favour I'll fairly venture
> Or that day I'll be where few kings enter.

Another ancient tale that entertained people for hundreds of years was

the exploits of George a Greene, the lusty Pindar of the North, which
was more usually known as The Pindar of Wakefield, vaguely set in the
times of Robin Hood. George gathered round him a band of his companions in Wakefield to defend the right. There are many stories of his
pranks, such as the one about Medle, the town busybody, who was a
thorn in everyone's flesh. George and his friends made a plot to put the
knave in his place. Accordingly, they held a great feast in Lent, to which
they invited Medle. During the course of the feast George saw Medle
slip some meat bones, wrapped in a cloth, in his pocket. George and his
companions plied Medle with drink and, when he was drunk, substituted
some fish bones for the others. As they had foreseen, the next morning
Medle informed on them to the magistrates for eating meat in Lent.
When asked for proof, since George denied it, Medle produced his
bundle of bones. The magistrates seeing they were fish bones, dismissed
the case, and away went Medle with a flea in his ear. Another story tells:

How George served a great Liar

There dwelt near to Wakefield a man that look what company soever he
came in, would tell the notablest lies, impossible to be believed. It chanced
this man to be in the company of George and his associates, and amongst
other talk, he began to tell what a great traveller he had been. Why, how
far? asked George. Why so far, that I did drive a tenpenny nail in the sky.
Why, said one, that is a lie. I think so, said another. Said George, I say it
is no lie, I do assure you it is a true tale: for I was on the other side and
clenched that nail. Judge you I pray you, did not he go beyond him in
his travels, as also in his lie? But, asked George, what have you seen in
your great travels? What, said he, why I have seen such huge cabbages in
Russia, that a hundred men and horses might have walked underneath
dry in a shower of rain. Whew, said one, here is a lie great indeed. I pray
you be content, said George, for I will tell you as strange a thing, but it
may be, that you will say it is a lie: I have seen such a huge cauldron made,
that there was an hundred men at work thereon; and those that were on
work driving in of the nails of one side, could not hear them on the other,
and when they would speak or call to one another, they had a trumpeter,
which should blow at that time his trumpet. Oh strange, said one; oh
strange, said another. I pray you, said the traveller, what was that cauldron
made for? Why truly Sir, said George, it was made only to boil your
cabbage. Whereat the company fell greatly alaughing, and the man was
so abasht, that he knew not what to do. But ever after this my traveller
would take heed how he told a lie in George's company.

In the later stories George and his band meet with Robin Hood and,
after a fight, the two companies of adventurers have a grand feast at

which several robust songs are offered, together with several more anecdotes, some of considerable interest.

One of the favourite jests that was reprinted many times was an anecdote about the Duke of Buccleugh:

Duke of Buccleugh

Henry, Duke of Buccleugh was greatly beloved by his numerous tenantry. One of his small tenants, Jamie Howie by name, had a son about four years of age, who, having heard much of a great Duke of Buccleugh, was very anxious to see him. Honest Jamie, in a few days, was honoured with a visit from the duke, when Jamie, doffing his bonnet, and making a reverential bow, says, 'O my Lord! ye maunna be angry wi' me, but it's God's truth, my Lord, there's a daft wee callant o' mine that canna rest, nor let others rest nicht nor day; he has ta'en in his head sic a notion o' seeing what like ye are, Gudesake, my Lord, I dinna think he has ony yedea ye are a man at a' but some far awa, outlandish, ower sea creature.' The Duke mightily tickled with his fancy, desired Jamie to bring the youngster into his presence forthwith. Out comes the juvenile inquisitor, with his finger in his mouth, and cautiously reconnitres the personage before him. At last quoth the urchin, 'Can ye soom?' 'No my little fellow,' replied his grace, 'I canna soom.' 'Can ye flee?' 'No, I canna flee.' 'Weel, man, for as muckle's ye-re I wadna gie ane o' my father's dukes for ye, for they can baith soom an' flee.'

3. Crime

Take warning, then, all ye as would
Not die like malefactors;
Never the company for to keep
Of them with bad characters.
Albert Smith

The reporting of crime was a staple of the chapbook and broadsheet industry. The well-to-do could read vivid accounts of the latest murders and robberies in the *Annual Register* and the *Gentleman's Magazine*; but even so, they shared also the more instant—if less accurate—versions produced by the printers nearby. And this busy trade flourished on both sides of the Atlantic. In 1787 the famous 'Abraham Panther' narrative was issued in Middletown, Connecticut, concerning a young woman who had been carried off by the Indians in 1777 and kept in the wilderness for nine years before she was at last brought back to civilization. The ever-present danger of sudden attacks by Indians was to haunt the Americans for many years afterwards—witness the case of the Barber family in Camden County, Georgia. There, on 26th January 1818 about forty Indians rushed the house and killed Darius Barber with tomahawks as he reached for his gun. They then tomahawked and scalped his children and a hired man, sacked the house and carried off his wife. After five weeks she managed to escape and return.

But the Indians were the subject of only some of the broadsheets that flowed from the American presses. There was Captain William Corran of the brig *Falmouth* who, in 1794, went berserk and hacked one of his passengers, Joseph Porter, to death with a cutlass. He was tried and executed at Halifax, Nova Scotia and, such was the intense interest in the case, a number of broadsheet accounts appeared in various parts of the country.

In England the case of the illegitimate Rebecca Downing, who was burnt at the stake in 1782, when she was only fifteen, is particularly moving. At the age of eight she was 'apprenticed' to the seventy-year-old Richard

31

Jarvis of East Portlemouth in Devon. Her tasks included removing weeds and stones from the fields, and tending the cattle. She is reported to have been indolent and sullen, and was frequently chastised. At her trial she was found guilty of poisoning her employer by putting arsenic in his breakfast potion of parched wheat prepared in the manner of coffee. It was Jarvis's grand-daughter who had accused her of doing this: she stated that when her grandfather became ill she tried to force Rebecca to drink a cup of the same liquid, but she spat it out. 'The girl confessed her guilt to the physician, and assigned a desire of being free from servitude as the motive.' In jail they found she knew nothing of Christianity and 'had never been told anything about having a soul'. 'Sometimes a tear would fall, but on the whole she seemed more stupefied than grieved by her situation. Here is the 'Lamentation' issued by T. Brice of Goldsmiths' Street, Exeter:

The Lamentation
of
Rebecca Downing

Condemn'd to be burnt at Heavitree,
near Exeter, on Monday, July 29, 1782,
for Poisoning her Mafter, Richard Jarvis.

GOOD People all, pray, pity me,
 And lift to my fad Tale.
From Birth the Child of Mifery,
 In Tears I now bewail.
Rebecca Downing is my Name;
 Of fenfual Parents born,
Who ne'er in holy Wedlock bound,
 Left me a Babe forlorn.

No tender Parent's fondling Kiſs
  E'er tun'd my Soul to Love;
No due Inſtruction taught my Feet
  In Virtue's Path to move.
In gloomy Ignorance I liv'd,
  Scarce glimps'd Religion's Light.
What wonder, when Temptation came,
  That I forſook the right?

Averſe to Labour's Drudgery,
  I ſigh'd for ſlothful Eaſe,
And with a Maſter's Murder thought
  To purchaſe quick Releaſe.
The mortal Poiſon with his Food
  I mix'd without Delay;
And now to ſatisfy his Blood,
  My Life for his muſt pay.

When to the fatal Stake I come,
  And diſſipate in Flame,
Let all be warn'd by my ſad Doom,
  To ſhun my Sin and Shame.
May I thus expiate my Crime,
  And whilſt I undergo
The fiery Trial here on Earth,
  Eſcape the Flames below.

The last public burning at the stake in England—again the criminal was
a woman—took place on 18th March 1789. Christian Bowman was deserted by her husband and lived with a coiner called Hugh Murphy.
They were both convicted at the Old Bailey for the high treason of
counterfeiting. Murphy was hanged. Christian Bowman was strangled
(she was hanging for forty minutes), and then burnt. By law, it was
provided that after 5th June 1790, condemned women should be hanged
in future.

Many crimes earned the capital sentence. In 1801 Henry Penson, 'a
person of considerable property' at Teignmouth in Devon, was sentenced
to die for sheep-stealing from one of his tenants. Penson denied the
accusation and, as the broadsheet reports, suggested in a written state-
ment to the court that his enemies must have hidden the various parts of
the sheep that were found all over his house. The jury remained un-
convinced.

Penson was not the only one to perish on the gallows at the New Drop,
Exeter, on 6th April 1801. Four more men were hanged for other cases of
sheep-stealing, a fifth for highway robbery, and a sixth for stealing beds

and hammocks from the Plymouth dockyards. With regard to the last man, the broadsheet reports his final words as:

All the sins I was guilty of, was giving to drunkenness and lewd women, and at last bad company did entice me to go with them to do this vile attempt, and for the same I now must die. But I hope the Lord has provided me with a resting place, where I shall dwell in endless joy. Amen.

The more farsighted printers kept in stock sets of woodcuts showing various numbers of criminals being hanged. In the case of Colonel Despard, however, the printer was defeated: his broadsheet shows six people on the gallows, but in fact there were seven. Marcus Despard (1751–1803), an Irishman and a good soldier, had an unhappy career in the Army. The unfairness of his treatment appears to have turned his head. He entered on a harebrained plot to assassinate the King and seize the Tower of London and the Bank of England. Along with his six conspirators he was drawn on a hurdle, hanged and then beheaded.

Pitts' broadsheet on the murder of Ann Williams in 1823 assured the readers that

> The bare relation of this deed
> Will make your blood run cold.

Ann Williams lived in service near Wirksworth in Derbyshire. She was seduced by a young man of twenty named William Jones. When she asked him to marry her, as he had promised, he took her for a walk:

> When to the fatal spot they came,
> These words to her did say:
> All on this very night I will
> Your precious life betray.
> On bended knees she then did fall,
> In sorrow and despair,
> Aloud for mercy she did call,
> Her cries did rend the air;

With clasped hands and uplift eyes
　　She cried, Oh spare my life,
I never now will ask you
　　To make me your wedded wife.
O then this wicked young man said,
　　No mercy will I show;
He took the knife all from his side,
　　And pierced her body through.
But still she smiling said to him,
　　While trembling with fear,
Ah! William, William, spare my life;
　　Think on your baby dear.
Twice more then with the bloody knife
　　He ran her body through,
Her throat was cut from ear to ear,
　　Most dreadful for to view;
Her hands and arms and beauteous face
　　He cut and mangled sore,
While down upon her milk white breast
　　The crimson blood did pour.
He took the shawl from off her neck,
　　And round her body tied,
With pebble stones he did it fill,
　　Thinking the crime to hide.
O then into the silver stream
　　He plunged her straightway,
But with her precious blood was stained,
　　Which soon did him betray.

In the same year occurred the murder of William Weare, of Lyon's Inn. This was a particularly brutal affair in which Weare perished at the hands of John Thurtell* (1794–1824), a fellow swindler and the son of a Norwich alderman. Catnach printed over a quarter of a million copies of the *Full, True, and Particular Account of the Murder*, and Pitts issued an equally impressive number of *The Confession and Execution of John Thurtell at Hertford Gaol:*

Exactly at two minutes past twelve [on Friday, 9th January 1824] the Under-Sheriff, with his wand, gave the dreadful signal—the drop suddenly and silently fell—and
　　　　JOHN THURTELL WAS LAUNCHED
　　　　INTO ETERNITY

* He appears in George Borrow's *Lavengro*.

The trial of Thurtell and his associates was but one more reminder of the large number of men and women in London who made their living out of the proceeds of all kinds of crime, retreating—when pursued—to the 'Holy Land', the rabbit-warren round St Giles where they were usually safe from arrest. A broadsheet of the period conveys the remarkable situation that existed before the introduction of Peel's New Police:

The Song of the Young Prig

My mother she dwelt in Dyot's Isle,
  One of the canting crew, sirs;
And if you'd know my father's style,
  He was the Lord *Knows-who*, sirs!
I first held horses in the street,
  But being found defaulter,
Turned rumbler's flunky for my meat,
  So was brought up to the halter.
Frisk the cly, and fork the rag,
  Draw the fogles plummy,
Speak to the tattler, bag the swag,
  And finely hunt the dummy.

My name they say is Young Birdlime,
  My fingers are fish-hooks, sirs;
And I my reading learnt betime,
  From studying pocket-books, sirs.
I have a sweet eye for a plant,
  And graceful as I amble,
Fine draw a coat-tail sure I can't,
  So kiddy is my famble.
Frisk the cly, &c.

A night-bird, oft I'm in the cage,
    But my rum chants ne'er fail, sirs,
The dubsman's senses to engage,
    While I tip him leg-bail, sirs.
There's not, for picking, to be had,
    A lad so light and larky,
The cleanest angler on the pad,
    In daylight or the darkey.
        Frisk the cly, &c.

And though I don't work capital,
    And do not weigh my weight, sirs,
Who knows but that in time I shall,
    For there's no queering fate, sirs.
If I'm not lagged to Virgin-nee,
    I may a Tyburn show be,
Perhaps a tip-top cracksman be,
    Or go on the high toby.
        Frisk the cly, &c.

Probably the biggest moneymaker of all the crimes was the murder of Maria Marten at the Red Barn. The story itself, one of seduction and promised marriage, was very similar to so many of that time, but the murderer—William Corder—was a remarkable man. Moreover after Maria's death her mother dreamt three times that the girl had been murdered and buried in Corder's Red Barn:

The Murder of Maria Marten

BY W. CORDER

Come all you thoughtless young men, a warning take by me,
And think upon my unhappy fate to be hanged upon a tree;
My name is William Corder, to you I do declare,
I courted Maria Marten, most beautiful and fair.

I promised I would marry her upon a certain day,
Instead of that I was resolved to take her life away.
I went into her father's house the 19th day of May,
Saying, my dear Maria, we will fix the wedding day.

If you will meet me at the Red-barn, as sure as I have life,
I will take you to Ipswich town, and there make you my wife;
I then went home and fetched my gun, my pickaxe and my spade,
I went into the Red-barn, and there I dug her grave.

ATROCIOUS MURDER OF A YOUNG WOMAN
IN SUFFOLK.
SINGULAR DISCOVERY OF THE BODY
FROM A DREAM.

THE RED BARN.

THE SCENE OF THE MURDER, AND WHERE THE BODY OF
MARIA MARTEN WAS FOUND CONCEALED.

With heart so light, she thought no harm, to meet him she did go
He murdered her all in the barn, and laid her body low;
After the horrible deed was done, she lay weltering in her gore,
Her bleeding mangled body he buried beneath the Red-barn floor.

Now all things being silent, her spirit could not rest,
She appeared unto her mother, who suckled her at her breast,
For many a long month or more, her mind being sore oppress'd,
Neither night or day she could not take any rest.

Her mother's mind being so disturbed, she dreamt three nights o'er,
Her daughter she lay murdered beneath the Red-barn floor;
She sent the father to the barn, when he the ground did thrust,
And there he found his daughter mingling with the dust.

My trial is hard, I could not stand, most woeful was the sight,
When her jaw-bone was brought to prove, which pierced my heart quite;
Her aging father standing by, likewise his loving wife,
And in her grief her hair she tore, she scarcely could keep life.

Adieu, adieu, my loving friends, my glass is almost run,
On Monday next will be my last, when I am to be hang'd.
So you, young man, who do pass by, with pity look on me,
For murdering Maria Marten, I was hang'd upon the tree.

Catnach sold well over a million copies of the broadsheet that included
these verses—he is thought to have written them himself!

Corder's execution outside Bury Gaol on 10th August 1828 drew an
immense crowd but, wherever a man or woman was due to suffer for a
crime, there was never any lack of spectators, and it was among these

ATROCIOUS MURDER OF A YOUNG WOMAN
IN SUFFOLK.
SINGULAR DISCOVERY OF THE 'BODY'
FROM A DREAM.
APPREHENSION OF THE MURDERER AT EALING, MIDDLESEX.

LIKENESS OF WILLIAM CORDER.

that the patterers found ready buyers for their wares. Thus at York, on 5th April 1830, the execution of William Shaw had many thousands of witnesses. Shaw had seduced Rachael Crossley of Kirkburton, near Huddersfield, and she troubled him by her constant importunities concerning marriage. At last he murdered her, and threw her body down a mineshaft:

The Kirkburton Tragedy, Giving an Account of the Murder of Rachael Crossley, of Kirkburton, near Huddersfield, by Wm. Shaw, her Sweetheart, also his Apprehension, and Execution at York, on the 5th of April, 1830.

Part I

Young Lovers all, pray now attend and listen unto me,
While unto you we do relate a dreadful tragedy:
Near Huddersfield a damsel liv'd, most beautiful and fair,
Untill by love she was betray'd, and drawn into a snare.

Rachael Crossley was her name, her stature was but small;
Her neighbours all around did her 'Little Rachael' call:
One William Shaw he courted her, and soon her heart beguil'd
To his desires she did give way, and then she prov'd with child.

He often vow'd he'd marry her, but as oft his vows did break,
Yet Rachael she did love him well, yes, for her infant's sake;
For four years more he courted her, and promis'd but in vain,
At length, to her misfortune, she prov'd with child again.

As they walked out one evening, she then to him did say,
'William, my dear, my time is near, pray fix our wedding-day.'
He said, 'My Little Rachael, pray cease to sigh and mourn,
We'll soon be publish'd in the church, and marry'd at Penistone.'

He did appoint the Ninth of March to walk with her that night,
To appoint their wedding-day, and put all things to right;
With joyful heart she met him, and through the fields did stray,
At a lonely place he seized her, and took her life away.

He said, 'Thou little harlot, thou ne'er shalt be my wife,
For here upon this very spot I'll take away thy life.'

Part II

Then he took her in his arms, and gave her a mortal wound,
'O! spare me and my babe,' she cry'd, and fell upon the ground.

In vain she scream'd, in vain she cry'd, to help her none was near
He said, 'No mercy I will shew, our wedding shall be here;'
He broke her skull and bruis'd her frame, and in gore she lay,
The babe he murdered in her womb, so took two lives away.

Her fair body he mangled, but still she was alive yet,
Near sixty yards he threw her down the shaft of a coal-pit;
When the Colliers went down this sight for to behold,
With amazement and horror it made their blood run cold.

Then poor Shaw was taken, and to York was sent with speed,
And at the Assizes he was try'd for this most cruel deed;
He was condemned to be hang'd upon the gallows tree,
His body to the Surgeons given dissected for to be.

So all young men whose heedless course fast to destruction run,
Repent in time while yet you may, and strive my fate to shun;
May my sad end cause you to mend, 'tis all that I do crave,
Least you like me hang on a tree, and never have a grave.

And for young Rachael's hapless fate, let pity drop a tear;
And may all youthful lovers mourn her destiny severe.
And now poor Shaw for this sad deed has undergone his doom,
Let us hope they both will meet where sorrows never come.

LIFE, TRIAL, CONFESSION, & EXECUTION

OF

JAMES GREENACRE,

FOR THE

EDGEWARE ROAD MURDER.

On the 22nd of April, James Greenacre was found guilty of the wilful murder of Hannah Brown, and Sarah Gale with being accessory after the fact. A long and connected chain of evidence was produced, which showed, that the sack in which the body was found was the property of Mr. Ward; that it was usually deposited in a part of the premises which led to the workshop, and could without observation have been carried away by him; that the said sack contained several fragments of shavings of mahogany, such as were made in the course of business by Ward; and that it contained some pieces of linen cloth, which had been patched with nankeen; that this linen cloth matched exactly with a frock which was found on Greenacre's premises, and which belonged to the female prisoner. Feltham, a police-officer, deposed, that on the 26th of March he apprehended the prisoners at the lodgings of Greenacre; that on searching the trowsers pockets of that person, he took therefrom a pawnbroker's duplicate for two silk gowns, and from the fingers of the female prisoner two rings, and also a similar duplicate for two veils, and an old-fashioned silver watch, which she was endeavouring to conceal; and it was further proved that these articles were pledged by the prisoners, and that they had been the property of the deceased woman.—Two surgeons were examined, whose evidence was most important, and whose depositions were of the greatest consequence in throwing a clear light on the manner in which the female, Hannah Brown, met with her death. Mr. Birtwhistle deposed, that he had carefully examined the head; that the right eye had been knocked out by a blow inflicted while the person was living; there was also a cut on the cheek, and the jaw was fractured, these two last wounds were, in his opinion, produced after death; there was also a bruise on the head, which had occurred after death; the head had been separated by cutting, and the *bone seemed nearly through*, and then broken off; there were the marks of a saw, which fitted with a saw which was found in Greenacre's box. Mr. Girdwood, a surgeon, very minutely and skilfully described the appearances presented on the head, and showed incontestibly, that the head had been severed from the body *while the person was yet alive*; that this was proved by the retraction, or drawing back, of the muscles at the parts where they were separated by the knife, and further, by the blood-vessels being empty, the body was drained of blood. This part of the

evidence produced a thrill of horror throughout the court, but Greenacre remained quite unmoved.

After a most impressive and impartial summing up by the learned Judge, the jury retired, and, after the absence of a quarter of an hour, returned into court, and pronounced a verdict of "Guilty" against both the prisoners.

The prisoners heard the verdict without evincing the least emotion, or the slightest change of countenance. After an awful silence of a few minutes, the Lord Chief Justice said they might retire, as they would be remanded until the end of the session.

They were then conducted from the bar, and on going down the steps, the unfortunate female prisoner kissed Greenacre with every mark of tenderness and affection.

The crowd outside the court on this day was even greater than on either of the preceding; and when the result of the trial was made known in the street, a sudden and general shout succeeded, and continued huzzas were heard for several minutes.

THE EXECUTION.

At half past seven the sheriff arrived in his carriage, and in a short time the press-yard was thronged with gentlemen who had been admitted by tickets. The unhappy convict was now led from his cell. When he arrived in the press-yard, his whole appearance portrayed the utmost misery and spirit-broken dejection; his countenance haggard, and his whole frame agitated; all that self-possession and fortitude which he displayed in the early part of his imprisonment; had utterly forsaken him, and had left him a victim of hopelessness and despair. He requested the executioner to give him as little pain as possible in the process of pinioning his arms and wrists; he uttered not a word in allusion to his crime; neither did he make any dying request, except that his spectacles might be given to Sarah Gale; he exhibited no sign of hope; he showed no symptom of reconciliation with his offended God. When the venerable ordinary preceded him in the solemn procession through the vaulted passage to the fatal drop, he was so overcome and unmanned, that he could not support himself without the aid of the assistant executioner. At the moment he ascended the faithless floor, from which he was to be launched into eternity, the most terrific yells, groans, and cheers were vociferated by the immense multitude surrounding the place of execution. Greenacre bowed to the sheriff, and begged he might not be allowed to remain long in the concourse; and almost immediately the fatal bolt was withdrawn, and, without a struggle, he became a lifeless corse.—Thus ended the days of Greenacre, a man endowed with more than ordinary talents, respectably connected, and desirably placed in society; but a want of probity, an absolute dearth of principle, led him on from one crime to another, until' at length he perpetrated the sanguinary deed which brought his career to so awful and disastrous a period, and which has enrolled his name among the most notorious of those who have expiated their crime on the gallows.

On hearing the death-bell toll, Gale became dreadfully agitated; and when she heard the brutal shouts of the crowd of spectators, she fainted, and remained in a state of alternate mental agony and insensibility throughout the whole day.

After having been suspended the usual time, his body was cut down, and buried in a hole dug in one of the passages of the prison, near the spot where Thistlewood and his associates were deposited.

This may well have been an unpremeditated crime: certainly the crowds at these executions discriminated between the differing degrees of guilt (as they saw it) in their reactions to the various criminals. For example, at the execution of the child-murderess, Mrs Winsor, the broadsheet reports:

> Thousands assembled in front of the gaol at a very early hour, and many had walked all night [to Exeter] to see the execution. Great commotion prevailed and it was evident that the crowd viewed the execution of a woman as a novelty, while they freely discussed the fiendish nature of the culprit, and expressed their total abhorrence of one who could make a business of murdering illegitimate offsprings. The horrible nature of the woman's crime (which needs not to be recapitulated here) so shocked the

better feelings of humanity, that when culprit and hangman stood side by side a fearful yell rose from the assembled crowd, and the excitement only ceased when the culprit, who struggled but little, ceased to exist.

In spite of the writer's promise, the circumstances were in fact recapitulated immediately below these words in the following verses;

Execution of Mrs Winsor

At Exeter,
For the barbarous murder of Mary Jane Harris's Child

You mothers all, come list to me,
 While a dreadful tale I tell,
Of all the crimes upon the earth,
 This one does all excel.
Children slaughter'd fearlessly,
And by a woman's hand,
Just for the sake of getting gold,
 This woman you command.

This dreadful woman, Charlotte Winsor,
 Took children in to nurse,
A devil she was in human form,
 We could not call her worse;
She would tamper with their young mother,
 With if you would like to pay,
For a few pounds, say three or four,
 I will put your child away.

Those children belong to some poor girl
 That had been led astray,
Mrs. Winsor would take them to nurse
 As long as they would pay.
She would murder them—yes, strangle them
 For this paltry gain,
By putting them between beds,
 Or pressing the juglar vein.

What must this wretch's feelings be,
 While the babes on her would smile,
She would kiss and feed him tenderly,
 And murder all the while.
She would tamper with their mothers,
 And of them beg and pray,
With get four pounds together dear,
 And your child shall die to day.

She stifled one just three weeks old,
    Jane Harris she would say,
You will never see them after,
    They will sink in the Torquay.
Dead children tell no tales,
    And cause no more strife,
And with children smiling on her,
    She would take away their life.

No one knows this woman's crime,
    But God's all seeing eye,
But justice overtook her,
    And for these crimes she died.
The tempter and the murderess,
    As you see by these lines,
Has gone to face their Maker,
    And to answer for her crimes.

The crowds never abated as long as public hangings continued to be held. Twenty thousand spectators, it is estimated, saw Thomas Oliver hanged, on Friday, 12th August 1836 for the murder of a farmer called May at Moretonhampstead. The broadside describes the crime:

Ye feeling hearted Christians, attend awhile to me,
While unto you I do relate a deed of cruelty;
A more attrocious murder you never heard before,
Than that of Mr. May, whose fate we now deplore.

Mr. May was a farmer, in Dunsford he did dwell,
And by his friends and relatives he was respected well;
He went to Morton fair, some cattle for to buy,
But ah! he little thought that he that night was doom'd to die.

When on his horse returning home he on the road was met,
By Oliver and Galley both on cruel deeds intent;
And then the life of Mr. May they quickly took away,
For which, upon the gallows high, their lives will dearly pay.

A frightful sight the body was, when found upon the road,—
His head all beat to pieces, and weltering in his blood;
His teeth knocked from their sockets, were strewed all around,
And clots of Mr. May's life-blood was trodden in the ground.

His body streaming in its gore, to Dunsford then was borne,
Where his poor friends heart-broken were waiting quite forlorn;
Their weeping neighbours pitied them, and went to soothe their grief
But, ah so deep their anguish was, they could gain no relief.

To prison drear, were Oliver and Turpin sent away,
With irons heavy they were bound to wait their trial day;
Stern justice then they feared to meet—their guilt was plainly seen,
That in the blood of Mr. May imbrued their hands had been.

Come all you wild and wicked men, think on the murder's fate,
Leave off your evil courses before it be too late,
O do not plunge yourselves in crime,—all bad examples shun,
Or you, like Oliver and Galley, may also be undone.

By now Sir Robert Peel's new police force had come into being, and was the subject of numerous ballads. The tone was mainly one of good-humoured banter, as in 'The Flower of the New Police, by Sally Spriggins, Spinster':

·THE RIGHTEOUS PEELER·

Oh! do not say of womankind,
    That a scarlet coat will enthral 'em;
If rags could enchant the fair ones thus,
    Rag fair ones you might call 'em.
I never was fond of the garb of war,
    Give me the robe of peace—
The deep, deep blue of X 41,
    The Flower of the New Police.
    *   *   *   *   *
I know I'se many rivals, love—
    There's three as lives next door,
And caps, I hear, are set at you,
    At number 44;
And I wish the maid at three-and-a-half
    Would please to hold her peace,
And not go telling lies of me
    To the Flower of the New Police.
She says I love you, single X,
    And double X, beside,

But that's all for to hinder you
From making me your bride.
Whate'er they say, my love for you
Will never, never cease,
So come to my arms, X 41,
Thou Flower of the New Police.

which is rather kinder than the comments on the many Irishmen who were recruited to the new force:

From Lim'rick's sweet city I came,
Without a shoe to my back, sir,
I carried a hod—what a shame!
But now I'm a gentleman, oh, wack, sir!
I'm dress'd in a neat suit of blue,
I'm so pleased that it will never cease, man,
And a shillelah I sport, too,
Because I'm a new policeman.

There was plenty of work for Peel's men to do. The murder and mutilation of the body of Celia Holloway by her husband caused a nationwide sensation. Catnach's contribution to the many broadsheets issued both in London and Brighton by the many printers willing to take advantage of the gruesome discoveries was a 'Lamentation and Confession of John William Holloway, who now lies in Horsham Gaol, awaiting his Trial for the Cruel Murder of his Wife:'

You tender-hearted Christians, I pray you now draw near,
And listen unto these few lines you quickly soon shall hear;
My name it is John Holloway, the truth I will unfold,
And when I think on what I've done it makes my blood run cold.

In Donkey Row I took a house, and there enticed my wife,
'Twas there by strangulation I took away her life;
An innocent babe all in her womb I murdered with my wife,
In pieces then I cut her up all with my bloody knife.

When I cut the body up—Oh! what a shocking sight
  Then on a barrow I wheel'd her to Preston in the night;
Her head and arms, her legs and thighs, from her body I cut off,
  Two thighs with her body I then buried in the Lover's Walk.

John Gillam, a fisherman belonging to Brighton town,
  And a constable from Preston soon the body found;
Oh! when the body was dug up, what a shocking sight to see,
  Her head and arms, her legs and thighs, were cut from her body.

And when the body was dug up some thousands flocked around,
  Then my wife's sister came and swore to her new stays and gown;
Then taken was Ann Kennett,* and put in close confined,
  And out of Brighton I did go, trying to ease my mind.

When back to Brighton I returned, thinking it was all right,
  But the God above was watching me and brought the deed to light,
Then taken was John Holloway and put in close confine—
  I am the wretched murderer, and must answer for my crime.

In these dark cells of Horsham gaol I cry both day and night,
  For the bleeding corpse of my poor wife is always in my sight:
When I hope her soul is in heaven at rest when I tormented I shall be,
  I deserve nothing but the Burning Flames for my sad cruelty.

Now young and old, pray beware of my unhappy fate,
  Pray let your Parsons comfort you before it is too late;
Hark! hark! I hear the dismal bell, how harsh it tolls—
  May the Lord have mercy on me and all poor unhappy souls!

LAMENTATION AND CONFESSION
OF
JOHN · WILLIAM HOLLOWAY,
WHO NOW LIES IN HORSHAM GAOL, AWAITING HIS TRIAL FOR
THE CRUEL MURDER OF HIS WIFE,
CELIA HOLLOWAY.

* his mistress.

In 1832 there was a particularly brutal murder of a young sailor at Enfield:

> This young man he was a sailor,
> And just returned from sea,
> And down to Enfield Chase he went
> His cousin for to see;
> Little thinking that ere night—
> Would prove his destiny.

The victim, Benjamin Crouch Danby, had been flashing his money too prominently in a public-house, and had been done to death by three local ne'er-do-wells. The new police, in their zeal, briefly arrested Charles Lamb, who lived close by and had been in the same inn that evening.

Broadsides about murders continued to be published for many years afterwards. On Sunday, 6th February 1853, a tax-collector and land surveyor called William Blackmore of Clayhidon in Devon was beaten to death for the sake of the money he was carrying. In addition to two poems (supposedly written by the accused) and a full account of the trial, the broadsheet prints the following letter from the condemned man, George Sparkes:

My dear Mother,

    I am now in the condemned cell, and must die for the murder of a good neighbour, and a kind friend Mr. Blackmore, I coveted his money, I did not intend to kill him, but you know I was going to get married and wanted to exalt myself above my station, but now wretch that I am, what disgrace my pride has brought me to, what anguish do I now feel, what disgrace upon my family, what sorrow to you my aged widowed mother, God help you, you taught me what was right, but I didn't hearken to it, for I took to gambling and drink, which ruined me, I murdered Mr. Blackmore, I am told I am to die next Friday, I hope the Lord will have mercy on my soul, I had none on Mr. Blackmore, Give my love to all my friends and brothers who I hope will forgive me, I am your wretched son

GEORGE SPARKES.

The Condemned Cell, March 25, 1853.

As late as 1879 a woman called Annie Took was arrested for the murder of a child. Reginald Hede had been deserted and was left in Annie Took's care. She had children of her own and there was no reason to fear any mistreatment of the orphan. When the boy disappeared, Annie Took said that two women had come to the house one day and had taken the child away, but suspicions were aroused, and orders were given for the millstream to be drained. At length several parts of the boy's body were recovered, and Annie sealed her fate by telling a number of other stories:

> The last scene is over of that awful crime,
> And Annie Tooke has now died in her prime—
> She has gone from this world with her sins on her head,
> For the Exeter murder she is now lying dead.
> Though artful and cunning, her time it was come,
> She had time to repent for what she had done;
> About this sad crime she told many a lie,
> It was all of no use she has now had to die.
>
> Annie Tooke is now dead and lies in her grave,
> For her poor children your pity we crave—
> The Exeter murder has now passed away,
> To the records of Heaven, and the judgment day.
>
> The child was deserted and left in her care,
> A sweet little boy so lovely and fair;
> One day it was missing, and then she did say,
> Two women had been there and took it away.
> But now we all know the body was seen,
> Cut into pieces and in the mill stream;
> She was then charged with this cruel crime,
> And this fearful deed brought to light in good time.
>
> She told many stories, they all were untrue,
> It was the worst crime a woman could do;
> We know every mother for a child ought to feel,
> And never so cruelly its dear life to steal.
> But all her false statements were of no avail,
> She was speedily taken and sent to a gaol;
> Her family at home in sad wretchedness,
> The Union before them in their deep distress.
>
> She lay in her cell awaiting her death,
> Dear life was going at each parting breath;
> Not a sound could be heard but the deep-toned bell,
> Of death drawing nearer each minute did tell.
> The months spent in prison came back to her mind
> And the fate of her children she has left behind;
> She thought of the day she committed the crime,
> Let us hope she repented while yet there was time.
>
> She trembled at death on that fatal morn,
> She knew that all chance of her life was gone;
> The hangman came to her and led her away,
> From the dark gloomy cell to the bright light of day.

The sweet birds were singing in full liberty,
Through the sweet winds of Heaven roaming so free;
The death knell sounds solemn and clear over head,
In a few seconds more Annie Took she was dead.

This should be a warning to one and to all,
Not to do that which we cannot recall;
Such crimes as these must be punished we say,
And answered to God on the great judgment day.
Thou shalt do no murder the Scripture doth say,
Or by man shall your life be taken away,
May God keep us all from such crimes as these,
And may we do nothing that will Him displease.

The gruesome gloating of so many of the bits of doggerel that accompanied these crimes is both astonishing and repellent to the people of today. Yet there were occasionally flashes of a keener understanding, and curiously enough one of the most impressive of these is an Irish ballad, which was reprinted again and again for almost two hundred years:

The Night Before Larry was Stretched

The night before Larry was stretched,
The boys they all paid him a visit;
A bait in their sacks too, they fetched;
They sweated their duds till they riz it:
For Larry was ever the lad,
When a boy was condemned to the squeezer,
Would fence all the duds that he had
To help a poor friend to a sneezer,
And warm his gob 'fore he died.

The boys they came crowding in fast,
They drew all their stools round about him,

Six glims round his trap-case were placed,
He couldn't be well waked without 'em.
When one of us asked could he die
Without having duly repented,
Says Larry, 'That's all in my eye,
And first by the clergy invented,
To get a fat bit for themselves.'

'I'm sorry, dear Larry,' says I,
'To see you in this situation;
And, blister my limbs if I lie,
I'd as lieve it had been my own station.'
'Ochone! it's all over,' says he,
'For the neck-cloth I'll be forced to put on,
And by this time to-morrow you'll see
Your poor Larry as dead as a mutton,
Because, why, his courage was good.'

'And I'll be cut up like a pie,
And my knob from my body be parted.'
'You're in the wrong box, then,' says I,
'For blast me if they're so hard-hearted;
A chalk on the back of your neck
Is all that Jack Ketch dares to give you;
Then mind not such trifles a feck,
For why should the likes of them grieve you?
And now, boys, come tip us the deck.'

The cards being called for, they played,
Till Larry found one of them cheated;
A dart at his napper he made
(the boys being easily heated);
'Oh, by the hokey, you thief,
I'll skuttle your nob with my daddle!
You cheat me because I'm in grief,
But soon I'll demolish your noddle,
And leave you your claret to drink.'

Then the clergy came in with his book,
He spoke him so smooth and so civil;
Larry tipped him a Kilmainham look,
And pitched his big wig to the devil;
Then sighing, he threw back his head,
To get a sweet drop of the bottle,
And pitiful sighing, he said:
'Oh, the hemp will be soon round my throttle,
And choke my poor wind-pipe to death.

'Though sure it's the best way to die,
Oh, the devil a better a-livin',
For, sure when the gallows is high
Your journey is shorter to heaven;
But what harrasses Larry the most,
And makes his poor soul melancholy,
Is to think on the time when his ghost
Will come in a sheet to sweet Molly—
Oh, sure it will kill her alive!'

So moving these last words he spoke,
We all vented our tears in a shower,
For my part, I thought my heart broke,
To see him cut down like a flower.
On his travels we watched him next day,
Oh, the throttler! I thought I could kill him;
But Larry not one word did say,
Nor changed till he came to 'King William'—
Then musha! his colour grew white.

When he came to the nubbling chit,
He was tucked up so neat and so pretty,
The rumbler jogged off from his feet,
And he lied with his face to the City;
He kicked, too—but that was all pride,
But soon you might see 'twas all over;
Soon after the noose was untied,
And at darky we waked him in clover,
And sent him to take a ground sweat.

4. History and Great Men

We are All tainted with the *Athenian* Itch,
News, and new Things do the whole World bewitch.
            Dr. Wild's Poem: *In nova fert animus, &c.*;
or, *A new song to an old friend from an old poet, upon
the Hopeful New Parliament. 1679.*

Comment on the events—national or local—of the day appeared in
every kind of form, and the catalogues of great libraries are full of entries
for pamphlets, squibs, broadsides, and other material which often landed
their writers, printers and distributors in gaol, and sometimes deprived
them of parts of their bodies. An early example was put out in 1676 by
Peter Folger, a Nantucket Quaker, under the title: 'A looking glass for
the Times. On the former spirit of New-England revived in this generation. To which is added, the Reports from the Lords of the Committee
of Councils, and the King's Order relating to the people called Quakers in
New England.' His spirited rebuke was addressed to the authorities at
Boston:

> Let all that read theſe Verſes know,
> That I intend ſomething to ſhow
> About our War, how it hath been,
> And alſo what is the chief Sin;
> That God ſo with us contend,
> And when theſe Wars are like to end,
> Read them in Love; do not deſpiſe
> What here is ſet before thine Eyes.

and has a curiously modern note. The American protest never ceased. In
1775, on 19th April General Thomas Gage (1721–87) sent the King's
troops to seize a quantity of arms at Concord. The next day there was the
battle of Lexington, and the American Revolution had begun: immediately a broadside entitled 'Bloody Butchery' was issued at Salem. The
next year Alexander Purdie printed at the Constitutional Post Office at

Williamsburg *The American Crisis*, in which he reminds his readers of
'the despotick inclinations' of James I:

> He muſt have ſuppoſed us to be a puſillanimous race of mortals, deſtitute
> of ſenſe and ſpirit, without the means of defending our injured rights,
> and unwilling to exert ourſelves in the defence of them.

Patriotism takes many forms; while the Americans were fighting for
their freedom, the British were equally involved in preserving their own.
On 12th April 1782 Rodney fought the French fleet under De Grasse, and
captured him and seven of his ships—a remarkable victory for which
Rodney was raised to the peerage. In 'Rodney Triumphant, and France
Humbled' occur the following verses:

> Kind heaven be pleas'd to protect all our fleets,
>   And fill each Britiſh tar with delight,
> And enſure them ſucceſs, whene'er on the ſea
>   For Old England's welfare they fight.
> May the church and the crown ſtand ever on earth,
>   Which to us a bleſſing muſt prove,
> May George our king, all his enemies fling,
>   Grant this, all ye powers above.
>
> So here is a health unto George our king,
>   And to Rodney and Hood here's the ſame,
> Hughes, Kempenfelt, Howe, Barrington and Roſs,
>   Prince William and Digby all fam'd.
> May each bold commander on ſea or on land,
>   While bravely oppoſing the foe,
> Put thouſands to flight, for Old England's right,
>   And conquer wherever they go.

Even in the midst of the most stirring events the minds of many men
were on purely local causes. In 1785 there was general consternation in
Exeter over spending on a new dock area by the Commissioners. 'Junius
Gingle' contributed a vigorous broadsheet, with an annotation: 'There
are a great many worthy Characters in the Commiſſion that have not
aſſiſted in the ſquandering away Nine Thouſand Pounds without an
Account, and nothing left to pay the Clerk, a Widow's Son, put in on
Purpoſe to help ſupport the Mother. About one-third of the Place is
unfiniſhed, and the worſt Third coſt no more than Seven Hundred
Pounds to pave it compleat.—This was not done in the Dock-Yard, nor
done by Yard Fellows.' His poem was entitled 'The Town in a Hurry;
or, The Dock Dance. A New Ballad', of which the following verses are
typical:

A contracting Commiſs'oner's loaves were found light;
One wanted two pounds and three ounces of weight;
And the other one pound and five ounces did lack,
Which proves this ſame Baker an infamous black.
    Then drive him thro' the town ſo, ſo drive him, &c.

        *   *   *

Dock-ſtreets were torn up to be better put down,
Which cauſed confuſion quite thorough the town;
For the ſtreets where theſe worthies did chuſe to reſide,
Tho' the beſt in the place, were new done thorough pride.
    But they can't go thro' the town ſo, ſo can't go thro' the town.

It is interesting to remember that this was happening in the same year that Francis Scott—of Washington County, Virginia—and his children were murdered by the Indians, and his wife taken captive by them; an account of which was published by John Trumbell at Norwich, Connecticut, in the next year. It is as though the inhabitants of the two countries were instead the inhabitants of two planets separated by millions of miles.

The struggles with the Indians continued remorselessly: there has survived a single copy of a broadside issued by Ezekiel Russell at Boston in 1791, concerning the overwhelming Indian defeat of the Governor of Ohio, General Arthur St Clair, and his troops near Fort Wayne, Indiana, when he tried to force the Indians to accept the provisions of the treaty of Fort Harmar. In France the Revolution was well under way, and in Ireland there were endless troubles, particular unrest being experienced in Cork at this time. When the Cork militia finally returned to their barracks, a most memorable poem was written which—in broadsheet form—passed from hand to hand and quickly became immortal:

De Groves of De Pool

Now de war, dearest Nancy, is ended,
    And de peace is come over from France;
So our gallant Cork city militia
    Back again to head-quarters advance.
No longer a beating dose rebels,
    We'll now be a beating de bull,
And taste dose genteel recreations
    Dat are found in de groves of de Pool.
        Ri fol didder rol didder rol, &c.

Den out came our loving relations,
    To see whether we'd be living or no;

Besides all de jolly ould neighbours,
    Around us who flocked in a row.
De noggins of sweet Tommy Walker,
    We lifted according to rule,
And wetted our necks wid de native
    Dat is brewed in de groves of de Pool.
        Ri fol, &c.

When de regiment marched into de Commons,
    'Twould do your heart good for to see;
You'd tink not a man nor a woman
    Was left in Cork's famous city.
De boys dey come flocking around us,
    Not a hat nor a wig stuck to a skull,
To compliment dose Irish heroes
    Returned to de groves of de Pool.
        Ri fol, &c.

Wid our band out before us in order,
    We played coming into de town;
We up'd wid de ould 'Boyne water',
    Not forgetting, too, 'Croppies lie down.'
Bekase you might read in the newses
    'Twas we made dose rebels so cool,
Who all tought, like Turks or like Jewses,
    To murther de boys of de Pool.
        Ri fol, &c.

Oh, sure dere's no nation in Munster
    Wid de groves of Blackpool can compare,
Where dose heroes were all edicated,
    And de nymphs are so comely and fair.
Wid de gardens around entertaining,
    Wid sweet purty posies so full,
Dat is worn by dose comely young creaturs
    Dat walks in de groves of de Pool.
        Ri fol, &c.

Oh! many's de time, late and early,
    Dat I wished I was landed again,
Where I'd see de sweet watercourses flowing,
    Where de skinners dere glory maintain:
Likewise dat divine habitation,
    Where dose babbies are all sent to school
Dat never had fader nor moder
    But were found in de groves of de Pool.
        Ri fol, &c.

Come all you young nouths of dis nation,
Come fill up a bumper all round;
Drink success to Blackpool navigation,
And may it wid plenty be crowned.
Here's success to the jolly hoop-coilers;
Likewise to de shuttle and de spool;
To de tanners, and worthy glue-boilers,
Dat lives in de groves of de Pool.
Ri fol, &c.

The reactions of the incessant wars are reflected too in an address 'To the Electors of Exeter', issued by T. Besley on 26th June 1802:

We have had ſure enough,
Of the War, and ſuch ſtuff;
With the bleſſing of peace we are favor'd once more;
And thoſe that muſt fight,
May 'njoy their delight,
By tranſporting themſelves to the African ſhore.

*   *   *

Then let us not ſwerve;
Independence we'll ſerve—
SIR CHARLES is our object, and that we'll purſue;
And I'll lay you a bet,
When Parliament's met,
There'll be COLONELS enough without any from you.

The sceptical attitude toward any naval or military man meddling in politics continued. In a broadsheet of 1812, the following satire is published:

Varmer & Dame

V.   Well Dame, and who do you vote vor, now than?
D.   Vote! why I cant vote atall, but my Husband can tho.
V.   And whichy way is he vor?
D.   He! why young Squire Whole-bones to be zure.
V.   Why vor such a Veller as he?
D.   Now I will tell he than.—You must know Varmer that I had a Zun that went to Zea, and was all that time in the zame Ship with the young Squire's Vather, and when I seedun agan he told ma and ma Husband Jan, how he would nit a come Home no more alive, if he hadden zarvd under old Maister; vor he zed good now, that his Maister, the old Squire, was nit alick other volks zich as How and Nelsin, vor when he zeed the Vrench, he hurnd away,

and was a veard to faitum, and zo a savd my Zun's Live—And zo
you know Varmer, that I and Jan be cruelly blidged to un, and
tharvore he'll gee his Zun a Vote.—And hurning away you know
is the best way of faiting now-a-days,—and zo old Maister thort.

V.   And zo I have a heard Dame.

D.   And vor this, he hav bin purmoted you know.

V.   Purmoted, what do ye maan?

D.   Why in the virst place, the volks changd old Maister's Name, and
calld un Admirble Whole-bones, and arter that Govarnment was
pleasd to gee un a Yeller Jacket, and vrom that time he was made a
Yeller Admirble.—And thats all I hav to zay about un.

Nevertheless, the British had a lasting pride in the military as long as
they kept to their own task. On 18th June 1815 the Battle of Waterloo
took place and put an end to the long struggle against Napoleon. This
was perhaps one of the most rewarding events for the printers of ballads
and chapbooks:

The Battle of Waterloo

At ten o'clock on Sunday the bloody fray begun,
It raged hot from that moment till the setting of the sun,
My pen, I'm sure, can't half relate the glory of that day,
We fought the French at Waterloo & made them run away.

On the 18th day of June, eighteen hundred and fifteen,
Both horse and foot they did advance, most glorious to be seen,
Both horse and foot they did advance, and the bugle horn did blow,
The sons of France were made to dance on the plains of Waterloo.

Our Cavalry advanced with true and valiant hearts,
Our Infantry and Artillery did nobly play their parts,
While the small arms did rattle, and great guns did roar,
And many a valiant soldier bold lay bleeding in his gore

and so on, for another fifteen verses of Catnach's best. Pitts, with as
lengthy a poem, did no better:

We followed up the rear till the middle of the night,
We gave them three cheers as they were on their flight;
Says Bony, d—n those Englishmen, they do bear such a name,
The beat me here at Waterloo, at Portugal, and Spain.

Now peace be to their honoured souls who fell that glorious day,
May the plough ne'er raise their bones nor cut the sacred clay;
But let the place remain a waste, a terror to the foe,
And when trembling Frenchmen pass that way they'll think of Waterloo.

Peterloo was a very different story. At an open-air meeting of the Manchester Reformists on 16th August 1819, addressed by Henry Hunt (1773–1835)—'Orator Hunt'—the very large crowd was charged by both yeomanry and cavalry. As a result a large number of people were injured, and some were killed:

Peterloo

See! see! where freedom's noblest champion stands,
Shout! shout! illustrious patriot band,
Here grateful millions their generous tribute bring,
And shouts for freedom make the welkin ring,
While fell corruption, and her hellish crew
The blood-stained trophies gained Peterloo.

At that time the elections brought forth new contributions from the agents:

A Cook's Song

TUNE – '*Moses and Vicar*'

Ye Farmers so bold,
Who Freeholds do hold,
Baron Cook your presence now craves,
To vote, Heart in Hand—
'BASTARD and ACLAND,'
And turn out young *Bother'em* GRAVES
Tol de rol, &c.

All *Lords* in the West,
My *Patrons* are blest;
But, Damme, I don't care a Fart:
I'll stick to Sir *Tom*,
As well as 'Squire *John*,
As long as I've Blood in my Heart.
Tol de rol, &c.

The Crediton *Snob*
Deserves well a Job:
Why then let him get a strong Rope,
And fix to a Tree,
To hang up this G.
Just like a November Pope.
Tol de rol, &c.

A New Song

TUNE – '*Snug Bit of Land in the Ocean*'

1.

NOW Election is near, thus in HONESTY's praiſe,
  Sing away, ſing away, then ſo clever;
For what man dare oppoſe this glad Toaſt which we raiſe,-
  'BENEVOLENCE!—VIRTUE! for ever.'
We're bound down by no Ties, but are Engliſhmen all,
  And in voting have all got a voice, boys;
All oppoſers on Poll-day muſt certainly fall;
  Vote away, vote away, vote away, then I ſay,—
    For good BULLER and GRANGER's our Choice, Boys.

2.

All the Poor they'll befriend, and of Orphans take Care,
  Sing away, ſing away, then, ſo ſtout, boys;
Let them ſee how reſolv'd, how determin'd we are,
  To put CHARLEY and N-T-N to rout, boys.—
Theſe well-wiſhers of Peace, and well-wiſhers of Trade,
  They have ſenſe full enough to direct us;
Why not ſpeak out our Minds, for, huzza! who's afraid?
  Vote away, vote away, vote away, then, I ſay,—
    Whilſt good BULLER and GRANGER protect us.

3.

When the Winter was hard, and all Ranks were diſtreſs'd,
  Sing away, ſing away, then, ſo jolly;
By a famine which reign'd, when the Poor were oppreſs'd,
  By dread hunger and ſad Melancholy;
Then good BULLER and GRANGER, they join'd hand in hand,
  For their Hearts were united together,
Each drew out his Purſe, for 'twas pity's Command,
  Vote away, vote away, vote away, then I ſay,—
    Let our GRATITUDE prompt us for ever.

The two examples just quoted are typical of the kind of propaganda published on the eve of an election, and it is hard to believe that they were distributed other than free to the few people who were in a position to vote at that time. The atmosphere of the Eatanswill Election in Dickens's *Pickwick Papers* is rife in the wording, and with the alteration of the names of the candidates such a poem could easily have been used for other election campaigns anywhere in the country.

The concern with local nepotism and mismanagement manifests itself in many of the broadsheets issued in the 1830s. At Exeter, in 1834, 'Diogenes Secundus' issued his *City Sketches*:

> Come gentle muse with step elastic,
> And dance a measure Hudibrastic;
> The strain shall be improvement's piers,
> And let the tune—to nature true—
> Be—'tickle me, I'll tickle you',
> I crave your pardon gentle muse,
> For putting you to such an use,
> I own they'r far 'neath your attention.

a preamble to a very lengthy account of the Commissioners' latest meeting. A more lively attack appeared two years later:

The Cod's Head-Council-Man *Connudated,*
OR
The Mer-Maids overflowing the *Bovey piss Pot*

> 'And Fishes beginning to *Sweat,*
> Cry Damme! how *hot* we shall be.'
>
> JOE MILLER.

TUNE: – '*Curse this vile* Tom Cat!' *or* '*Lunnun is the Devil*'.

> What a rout and fuss!
> Is made by c***** s*****be,
> About our *Poissoniers*:
> Who threats he'll *split* or *Burke* em;
> Now all this hate d'ye see,
> In story—short or long Sir,
> Is—'cause they *catechise*
> Such *Sneaks* in *Vulgar Tongue* Sir.

> Clampy—feels disgust
> At CHOUTERS lack of Morals,
> Like Mawworm *whites* his Eyes,
> And groans 'The filthy quarrels.
> 'Of those Women vile
> 'In TRAWLING slang mysterious,
> 'Infect all standers-by
> 'With Language *deleterious*.'

> 'Down—they must be put
> 'And *Whaling Saints* supported,

'Such as will loud grunt,
'*Dutch Anthems* just imported.
'Fresh as *Herrings red,*
'Or *Citrics* from OPORTO,
'Figs and *Flanders-Bricks,*
'And Nuts of every sort-O.'

BULL CALF'S *ventral* fat
Praises well his Table
Like HERC'LES he can *hug,*
A FISH FAG!—broom a Stable!
Ravish Venders too,
Of *Cockles—Shrimps,* and *Dories;*
On BABY CLOTHS descant
And vote against the TORIES.

Lady BARTLETT says—
's******e you're a Tunny!
'Then bids him kiss her Arse!
'In accents far from funny;
'In CLOVERS—sharp you are
'Although in *Fish*—a *Flat* Sir!
'As certain—as I've got
'A Hole in MY OLD HAT Sir.'

FRY him BROWN ye Nymphs—
Laver him with blessings,
CRIMP him too with COD,
And *Conger Guts*—sweet messings,
Stinking Dabs and *Skate,*
Putrid *Soles* and *Whiting,*
Sound him with your *Tongues,*
But—keep your *Fins* from STRIKING!
ICHTHYOPHAGOS.

With the accession of Queen Victoria, much of the attention of the ballad-writers was turned to the royal family—which is discussed in another chapter. Politics, too, had their fair share, but there was no sign of the sophisticated treatment which the French had been giving to such matters for at least the preceding hundred years. The tendency was, instead, to keep to the familiar pattern of tub-thumping; and the humour, where it existed, was of a very crude and obvious variety. The approach was, in fact, very much that of the modern political cartoonist who would be loath to separate a Stanley Baldwin from his pipe, or a Neville Chamberlain from his umbrella. Occasionally, a national event outside the Court's ambience bound the nation in a feeling of unity, and an outstanding example of this was the death of the Duke of Wellington in 1852:

Death of The Duke of Wellington

BORN	DIED
May 1st. 1769	Septr. 14 1852

O Britons give ear to these lines I relate,
    There was never a General more bolder
The leader in war, the pilot in state,
    A noble and gallant old soldier;
Respected, revered, beloved too & feared
    No tyrant did e'er dare molest him,
He is gone, he is dead, his bold spirit hath fled,
    The Duke of Wellington's gone and God rest him.

In the councils of state, of old England's fate
    Our Queen he did oft call upon her
He is gone we may see aged near 83,
    Full of age full of glory and honour,
He fought and he conquer'd in France, & in Spain,
    No power on earth could molest him,
And at great Waterloo, he made Boney to rue
    But he now is no more and God rest him.

He at Walmar did die, in his shroud he doth lie
    The glory and pride of Britannia,
He made tyrants to quake and the world for to shake,
    Our gallant and noble commander:
He was never seen fret death and danger he met
    And the friends of Britannia oft bless'd him
He has gone to that home where he'll never return
    Our gallant old Duke God rest him.

He never fear'd wars alarms when the drum beat to arms
    He acted bold upright and steady
He in glory would rage, the foe to engage
    To conquer or die he was ready
A true gallant soldier of fame and renown
    As a General well did adore him
He made tyrants relent wherever he went
    And Emperor's trembled before him.

Death sent him a summons to call him away
    From the Castle of Walmar near Dover
He resign'd when it came all his honour & fame
    And said now the battle is over:

The enemies weapons he boldly defied,
    They trembled and fear'd to molest him
In honour he lives in glory he died,
    The Duke he has gone, God rest him

In sad anguish so deep, Victoria did weep
    When the tidings Britannia sad told her
She in grief did deplore, and she said never more,
    Will Britannia behold her old soldier.
Long in famed history, he recorded shall be,
    In the garment of death they have laid him
In glory & fame he'll no more march again
    Our noble old Duke, God rest him.

THE MAN WOT DRIVES THE SOVEREIGN.

The day of the broadsheet was now drawing to a close, apart from its use in local issues. Occasionally there would be an event large enough to inspire a printer to put out a leaflet of the old type. This was the case in connection with the murder of Lord William Russell, who was killed by his Swiss valet, François Benjamin Courvoisier, in 1840. The style had changed: two thirds of the sheet were devoted to summaries of the verdict, the sentence, and the execution, while the last part offered an 'Affecting Copy of Verses':

    Oh hark! what means that dreadful sound?
        It sinks deep in my soul;
    It is the bell that sounds my knell,
        How solemn is the toll.

See thousands are assembled
Around the fatal place,
To gaze on my approaching,
And witness my disgrace.

There is no need to repeat the other verses, similarly banal, for it is clear that the words were written by the worst of hacks. Better to give the text of a remarkable little drama which made its appearance in 1857:

A Little Play,
Entitled
'The Rejected Candidate'

(The Rejected Candidate has met his sympathizing Friends,
and the Meeting, broken up, came out as they went in.)

A SCENE IN THE STREET

A Common-Sense Man—(RALPH S*****S.) My Friends, the Meeting spoke plain, there were not Ten sincere Men in the room—the sympathy was for their Shops—the cold austere manner of D. was offensive, yea, insulting to Gentlemen; he walked, as if he honored the City, not the City him. I have no regret—

A Warm-hearted Charitable Man, but very Peppery—(BOB C*****H.) Was not the grey-whiskered Barber sincere? (Cries of no!—The shop, to please his Aristocratic Customers.) Was not Old Document the Lawyer? (Shouts of laughter.) Bob, very excited—You will next say that the Parsons were insincere.

A Puseyite Priest—(FATHER KIT. B*********W.) The Church was very sincere; I did all I could for the cause. Oh! that Rougemont Traitor.

Old Billy, Blunt Man—(BILLY H****R.) The doings of sich like thee, would damn any honest man.

The last rejected Candidate for South Devon—(SIR S. N*******E. Aside, to a Fine Old Gentleman—JOHN C***W.) Truer than Gospel, he and that lot damned me in the South—

FINE OLD GENTLEMAN. (Aside.) They will in the North.

FATHER KIT. I have a mind to say that should the Evil One appear I would forsake thee.

OLD BILLY. I knows that thee art Chums, therefore us, will not offend thee.

FINE OLD GENTLEMAN. Betwixt you and me, Common Sense, the true regret is that a few select can no longer dictate.

Old Satan—(JACKDAW.) (A strong smell of sulphur, accompanied with loud and odd sounds.—Father Kit trembles and looks pale.—Old Satan appears.) You blundering fools, I did the mischief, being fond of fun.

FATHER KIT.—The Devil.—(Runs away.) All run different ways, leaving.

SOLILOQUY.

OLD SATAN. (Rubbing his hands with delight.) The G.C.P. scattered to the winds.—Who will collect them again? Not LITTLE TOM!!!

Tempora mutantur, et nos mutamur in illis.

The last offering in this sad tale of the decline of the broadsheet was issued some years after the introduction of the Education Act of 1870. This extraordinarily ugly piece of bombastic printing was issued at Exeter on 3rd December 1873, and could only have been the product of a man singularly lacking in sensibility:

To the
Electors of Exeter

S ilver, copper, brass in plenty,
I n my pockets mix with gold;
R ailway Shares enough for twenty,
E ndless wealth and power untold.
D ividends at all the quarters,
W ondering Clerks my Agents pay;
A rtisans and Guards and Porters,
R ailways three my word obey.
D oubt not I can help you greatly,
W ork for thousands I can bring,
A nd with Parks and Mansions stately,
T ry to prove a 'Railway King'.
K now that I am now Director,
I n the Chair of Railways three,
N ever was so great Protector,
K ing or Kaiser, Pope, as me.
N ow's your chance, my wise Elector,
T ake me for your new M.P.

SIR EDWARD W. WATKIN, KNT.

S.E.R., M.S. & L.R., AND M.R.

5. Courtship & Marriage

Farewell, my Love, since he is gone,
I like a Turtle for him will mourn.
True Love is like the raging Seas,
Tost up and down I take no Ease.
        *The Maid's Lamentation for Loss
        of Her Shepherd*

The armed field of love is one of the most attractive features of street literature. The chapbooks had little to contribute, beyond spells to reveal the identity of the future spouse, models of the high-flown letters with which one could entertain a favoured suitor or reject out of hand an unsuitable rascal, and the occasional crude wooing that stemmed from even broader stories of the middle ages. But the broadsheets were often devoted to affecting tales of love spurned, trust deceived, wooing trifled with, and lovers lost on the high seas, in battle, or without a trace. There was 'The Sorrowful Lamentation of Miss Sarah West' in 1782, the story of an unhappy young lady who lost her life with her sweetheart on board the *Formidable*, man-of-war commanded by the brave Rodney, in the engagement with De Grasse: Her lover was pressganged; as soon as she heard of this Sarah West disguised herself as a man. The lovers served together and, in battle, Sarah was mortally wounded. Her lover, horror-stricken and distraught, seized her lifeless corpse and leapt with it into the ocean 'amid the tears and lamentation of his brave companions'.

Earlier poems could be light-hearted:

A Spell for Ione

Tell me, sweet girle, how spellst thou Ione?
    Tell me but that, is all I crave,—
I shall not neede to lye alone,
    When such a lovely mate I have.
That thou arte one who can denye,
    O one whose praise no tonge can tell?
And all will graunt that I am I,—
    O happy I, if right thou spell:—
If I am I, and thou art one,
Tell me, sweete wench, how spelt thou Ione?

Ile tell you, sir, and tell you true,
    For I am I and I am one,
So can I spell Ione without you,
    And spelling so, can lye alone:
My I to one is consonant,
    But as for yours, it is not so:
If then your I agrement want,
    I to your I must aunswer no;
Wherefor leave of your spelling plea,
And let your I be I *per se.*

Your aunswer makes me almost blind,
    To put out one and leave one I;
Unless herein some hope I find,
    Therefor I must dispayre and dye;
But I am you, when you doe speake;—
    O speak againe, and tell me so!
My hart with sorrow cannot break
    To heare so kinde a graunting, no;
For this is all for which I sue,
That I may be turnd into you.

Nay, if you turne and wind and press,
    And in the cross-row have such skill,
I am put down, I must confess;
    It bootes me not to cross your will.
If you speak tru, say I stand to it,
    For you and I are now but one;
And I will ly that you may doe it,—
Now put together we spell Ione:
But how will Ione be speld, I wonder,
    When you and I shall part asunder?

Common though such a standard of writing was in the seventeenth century, it was rarely to be found in the next two hundred years in the many broadsheets that recounted the various ways of courting a maid. One of the most popular of the more humorous accounts of wooing occurs again and again in different forms, and was clearly very well known all over the country:

The Taylor's Courtship

When Harry the taylor was twenty years old
He began to be gamesome courageous and bold
He told his mother he was not in jest,
For he would have a wife as well as the best.

In the morning a little before it was day
To the house of a farmer he straight took his way
Where he found the maid Dolly a making of cheese
He began for to kiss and tickle her knees.

The girl in a rage offended at that
Cried you young rascal what would you be at,
He said dear Dolly I'll make you my wife
For I love you as well as I do my own life.

Tho' I am a taylor tis very well known
I have the choice of young Nancy Kate Bridget & Joan
I slighted them all for sweet Dolly my dear
And besides I've a house of five shillings a year.

O thou pitiful soul thou shall soon understand
There is never a pilfering thief in this land
Shall once have the fortune to lay by my side
Then straight with a churn staff she well lac'd his hide

A bowl full of butter milk on him she threw
He began to be vexed and look wonderful blue
Said he dear Dolly what have you done
Down my back thru' my breeches good faith it doth run.

She push'd him in anger he tumbled he fell,
From the door of the dairy down into the well,
Then Harry cried out with a sorrowful sound,
Help me out Dolly or I shall be drown'd.

Roger hearing a roaring came out in a maze,
And soon help'd him up in a bucket again,
Crying out zounds what brought you here,
It was Dolly threw me in honest friend I declare.

She said dear Roger observe what I say,
He came in the morning before break of day,
And I was at work in the dairy alone,
He made free with that which was none of his own.

Then the taylor went home like a poor drown'd rat
Telling his disaster and what he'd been at,
Of the butter-milk bowl and the desperate fall,
And if these be love's tidings the deuce take them all.

This is very different from a rare poem that appeared in a curious series
of halfpenny pamphlets, about half the size of the average chapbook,
which was issued in Scotland at the beginning of the nineteenth century,
and usually included two or three poems printed on very rough grey
paper:

Mrs. Runnington's Wig

Mistress Runnington wore a wig,
 Contrived to peep at a man,
And every feature to twig,
 As commode as the sticks of a fan.
For the book of her labour and her cares,
 Now drew pretty near the last page;
And this wig had a few griz'y hairs,
 That escaped from the avarice of age.
Mister Doddington—Oh, a nice man,
 Rather old, and a little a prig,
Fell in ecstasy, stark staring mad,
 With sweet Mistress Runnington's wig.

Mr. Doddington wore a wig,
 To hide his poor head so crazy;
'Twas neither too little nor big,
 Nor so much a wig as a jasey;
But he wheezed pretty much with a cough
 And, being long since past his prime,
He looked, when the jasey was off,
 Exactly the figure of time.
Mrs. Runnington fell in the snare,
 Thus laid by this amorous sprig;
Believing 'twas natural hair,
 As he did Mistress Runnington's wig.

His [*sic*] kiss'd her, the bargain to strike,
 For they both had agreed on the match,

When the wire-work of her vandyke,
  Caught the buckle that fastened his scratch.
In vain they both struggled and grinned,
  'Twas useless to labour and pull,
Their nappes as tightly were pinned,
  As a dog at the nose of a bull.
At length both the fabrics crazy,
  By a resolute effort, and big,
Down fell Mr. Doddington's jasey,
  And poor Mrs. Runnington's wig.

Now, as bald as my hand or two cootes,
  They stood petrified at the disaster;
But it soon finished all their disputes,
  And tied their affection the faster.
Each admiring the other's good sense,
  Made the best of their dismal miscarriage
And alleged in their mutual defence
  Secrets ne'er should be kept before marriage;
Though they look'd like two monkies run crazy,
  While they laugh'd at the frolicksome rig.
She restored Mr. Doddington's jasey,
  And he Mrs. Runnington's wig.

Some of the poems that were issued in broadsheet form were sufficiently equivocal to have puzzled even the readers of those times. The following song is a typical example:

The Chearful Wife

I once was a Maiden as freſh as a Roſe,
  And as fickle as April weather,
I laid down without care, and wak'd with repoſe,
  With a heart as light as a feather.
                    With a heart, &c.

I work'd with the girls, and play'd with the men,
　　I always was romping or ſpinning;
And what if I pilfered a kiſs now and then,
　　I hope 'twas not very great ſinning.
　　　　　　　　　I hope, &c.

I wedded a huſband as young as myſelf,
　　And for every frolick was willing,
Together we laugh'd when we had any pelf,
　　And we laugh'd when we had not a ſhilling.
　　　　　　　　　And we laugh'd, &c.

He's gone to the wars—heav'n ſend him a prize,
　　For his pains he is welcome to ſpend it;
My example I know is more merry than wiſe,
　　Lord help me—I never ſhall mend it.
　　　　　　　　　Lord help me, &c.

the cynicism of which is echoed in an Irish song of the eighteenth
century:

The Rakes of Mallow

AIR – '*Sandy lent the man his Mull.*'

Beauing, belling, dancing, drinking,
Breaking windows, damning, sinking,
Ever raking, never thinking,
　　　　　　　Live the rakes of Mallow.

Spending faster than it comes,
Beating waiters, bailiffs, duns,
Bacchus's true begotten sons,
　　　　　　　Live the rakes of Mallow.

One time naught but claret drinking,
Then like politicians thinking
To raise the sinking funds when sinking
    Live the rakes of Mallow.

When at home with dadda dying,
Still for Mallow water crying;
But where there's good claret plying
    Live the rakes of Mallow.

Living short but merry lives;
Going where the devil drives:
Having sweethearts, but no wives,
    Live the rakes of Mallow.

Racking tenants, stewards teasing,
Swiftly spending, slowly raising,
Wishing to spend all their days in
    Raking as at Mallow.

Then to end this raking life
They get sober, take a wife,
Ever after live in strife,
    And wish again for Mallow.

The usual tales of seduction and desertion, very often told mechanically and without any real appreciation of the distress they recounted, occasionally included one with rather more approach to real life. Even their sensationalism affords glimpses of a world where a woman, on first conviction for stealing, could be transported to Botany Bay for fourteen years. The account of Elizabeth Watson reminds one too that those who were sent to penal servitude in Australia could be returned also, and that the 'hulks'—of which there is so vivid a description in *Great Expectations* —saw scenes of cruelty and degradation which continued until a little over one hundred years ago. The following effort of Catnach's is therefore reprinted in full:

The Remarkable, Affecting, and Interesting LIFE, and Dreadful Sufferings of the poor unhappy

ELIZABETH WATSON

The Daughter of a wealthy Merchant near Piccadilly, who was

Seduced by a Gentleman,

Under a promise of Marriage, at the early age of Sixteen, who afterwards abandoned her to all the horrors of infamy and poverty. Her Father refused her admittance to his house, and She was cast upon the Town, where, after enduring all the miseries of Prostitution, she was tempted through extreme distress to Rob her landlady, for which she was convicted at the Old Bailey, and

Transported to Botany Bay

Shewing the

DREADFUL HARDSHIPS

Which she underwent for Fourteen Years. Concluding with her return to England, a sincere Penitent, where she was kindly received by her Father.

J. Catnach, 2, Monmouth-court, 7 Dials

> Ye British maids pray lend an ear
> While I with pain unfold
> A tale most sorrowful to hear,
> Yet true as e'er was told.
> A merchant's daughter I was born,
> Of very good degree,
> And how I was reduc'd to scorn,
> You presently shall see.
>
> I tender parents did possess,
> Who cherished my youth,
> They reared me with tenderness
> In virtue and in truth.
> No sorrow then my bosom knew,
> My heart was light and free;
> But soon these happy moments flew
> Sad was the change to me.
>
> When I was fifteen years of age,
> My tender Mother died,
> No soothing could my grief assuage,
> Most bitterly I cried.
> She clasp'd me in her dying arms,
> And strict advice she gave,
> To guide my steps, & keep from harm
> When she was in her grave.
>
> Soon after this a gentleman,
> Did gain my virgin love,
> My youthful heart he did trepan,
> And vow'd by all above,
> That I should be his wedded wife
> Before a month went round,
> And be a Lady fix'd for life,
> The richest in the town.

His artful tongue did me decoy—
　　My Father's house I left:
Each sinful pleasure did enjoy—
　　Most stylish was I kept.
But e'er a twelvemonth was elaps'd,
　　I found myself betray'd;
He left me plunged in distress,
　　For all the vows he made.

Distracted with his conduct base,
　　Disconsolate and poor;
My Father would not see my face,
　　But spurn'd me from his door.
I wander'd weeping up and down,
　　Till almost famished,
And at length was forc'd upon the town,
　　For miserable bread.

My landlady was very kind,
　　While I had health to please,
But all her friendship prov'd but wind,
　　When dying with disease.
She turn'd me out into the street,
　　All shivering and pale,
Without one bite of food to eat,
　　And none would hear my tale.

Thus pass'd six dreary months away
　　Midst want and poverty,
Till I upon a fatal day,
　　Was drove to felony.
Straight unto Newgate was I sent,
　　My sentence to await;
And there did bitterly lament
　　My poor unhappy fate.

The Judge declar'd my guilt was clear
　　So I was doom'd straightway,
To be transported fourteen years,
　　O'er seas to Botany Bay.
Unto which place I went with speed,
　　Along with many more,
Whose heavy hearts with grief did bleed
　　To leave their native shore.

Full fourteen years I did remain,
　　And when my time expir'd,

To England I return'd again,
    Which was my heart's desire.
Our ship was wrecked on the way,
    And sixty found a grave,
But I upon the wreck did stay,
    And Heaven did me save.

My aged Father long had mourn'd,
    As tho' that I were dead;
But when he heard I had return'd,
    What floods of tears he shed.
No longer he would me disown,
    His anger died away,
And took the weary wanderer home,
    Who long had gone astray.

Ye maids while beauty's in its prime,
    Of perjur'd youths beware,
Who oft with studied, base design
    Deceive the easy fair.
Tis sweet to view, when May has drest,
    The fair and flow'ry brake,
But ah! beneath its rosy vest
    It hides the vengeful snake.

The question must often have arisen in the ballad reader's mind as to what happened to all these lovers who deserted their too trustful mistresses. The answer is at least partly provided in Daft Watty's tale:

Daft Watty's Ramble to Carlisle

If you axe me where I come frae, I say the fell syde,
Where fadder and mudder and honest fowk beyde,
And my sweetheart—O bless her!—she thought nyen like me,
For when she shuik hands the tears gush'd frae her e'e.
Says I 'I mun e'en get a spot if I can,
But whate'er betide me, I'll think o' thee, Nan!'

SPOKEN—Nan was a perfect beauty, wi' twee cheeks like codlin blossoms; the verra feet on her made my mouth a' water. 'Faree-te-weel, Watty!' says she, 'tou's a wag amang lasses, and I'll see thee nae mair.' 'Nay, dunnet gow, Nan,' says I—

'Fo mappen, or lang, I'se be maister mysel;'
Sae we buss'd, and I tuik a last luik at the fell.
On I whussel'd & wander'd: my bundle I flung
O'er my shoulder, when Cowley he oftea my sprung,

An' howl'd, silly fellow! an' fawn'dat my fit,
As if to say –Watty, we munnet part yet!
At Carrel I stuid, wi' a strae i' my mouth,
And they tuik me, nae doubt, for a promisin youth;—

The weyves com round me in clusters—'What weage dus te ax, canny lad?' says yen. 'Wey, three pun and a crown; wunnet beate a hair o' my beard.' 'What can te dui?' says anudder. 'Dui! wey, I can plough, sow, mow, shear, thresh, dike, milk, kurn, muck a byer, sing a psahlm, mend car-ger, dance a whornpype, nick a nag's tail, hunt a brock, or feight iver a yen o' my weight in aw Croglin parish.'

An auld bearded hussy suin caw'd me her man;
But that day, aw may say't a' my sorrows began.

Furst, Cowley, poor fellow! they hang'd i' the street,
And skinn'd, God forgi'e them, for shoon to their feet;
I cried, and they caw'd me peur half-witten clown,
And bantered and follow'd me all up and down;
Neist my deam she e'en starv'd me, that ever liv'd well,—
Her hard words and luiks wad hae freeten'd the de'il.

She had a lang beard, for aw t'war' like a billy goat, wi' a kiln-dried frosty face; and then the smawest leg o' mutton in a Carel market served the cat, me, and her for a week. The bairns meade sec gam on us, and thundered at the rapper as if to waken a corp; when I opened the duir, they stour i' my e'ed, and caw'd me daft Watty—

Sae I pack'd up my duds when my quarter was out,
And, wi' weage i' my pocket, I saunter'd about.

Suin my reet han' breek pocket they picked in a fray,
An wi' fyfteen white shillings they slipp'd clean away;
Forbye my twee letters that com' frae mudder an Nan,
Where they said Carel lasses wad Watty trepan;
But 'twad take a lang day just to tell what I saw,
How I 'scap'd frae the gallows, the swodgers and a'.

Ay, there were some forgery chaps bid me just sign my neame. 'Nay,' says I, 'you've gotten a wrang pig by the lug, for I canna write!' Then a fellow like a' leaced an' feathered, ax't me, 'Watty, wull te list? Thou's either be a general or gomeral.' 'Nay, I winnet, that's plain; I'se content wi' a cwot o' mudder's spinnin.'

Now, wi' twee groats and tuppence, I'll e'en toddle heame,
But ne'er be a swodger while Watty's my neame.
Now my mudder 'll gowl, and my fadder 'll stare,
When I tell them poor Cowley they'll never see mair;

Then they'll bring me a stuil,—as for Nan, sh'll be fain,
To see I'm return'd to my friends yence again;
The barn and the byer, and the auld hollow tree,
Will just seen like cronies yen's fidgin to see;

The sheep'll nit ken Watty's voice now! The peat-stack we used to lake
round'll be burnt ere this! As for Nan, she'll be owther married or broken-
hearted! An' aw be weel at Croglin, we'll hae sic fiddlin; dancin', drinkin',
singin' and' smoakin', till aw's blue about un—

Amang aw neybors see wonder I'll tell,
And never mair leave my auld friends or the fell.

6. Trades and Professions

So for Traders and Merchants, I care not a fig—
I'll sing, and I'll laugh, and I'll dance out my jig.
An Answer to the Song of Banter

Up to the beginning of the nineteenth century the general curiosity of everyone with regard to each other's calling was intense, and vague designations such as 'something in the City' would certainly have been pursued by further questions. The Veneerings and their many colleagues were a product of a slightly later age, and coincided with the acceleration of growth of the population and the rapid industrialization of the country. It was not of course always necessary to ask a man's trade; as the various illustrated editions of the popular Cries of London have demonstrated, many a man could be identified for what he was by the clothes he wore, or the tools he carried. The unfortunate barber of the seventeenth century who was buried beneath one of the stones of Avebury as he ran across the street could not have been mistaken for any other. Equally, in the professions, there were sufficient signs to enable people to distinguish easily between the apothecary and the parson, the lawyer and the nonconformist minister.

The Cries of London have an eternal fascination, for they carry with them not only the very real seal of authenticity in their references to things long since past, but they also remind the reader of things that have vanished within his own lifetime: the muffin man with his bell, the German band on the corner, and the incessant cries of 'any old rags?'—for which one was likely to receive in return a potted geranium in full flower:

The Trader's Medly; or The Crys of London

TUNE – *When Cold Winter Storms are past.*

Holly & Ivy or Missleto,
Do you want any Greens your Houses to strow,

78

THE

Cries of London.

Milk below.

Cherries.

Here's round and sound,
Black and white heart cherries,
Two-pence a pound.

Rain, frost, or snow, or hot or
cold,
I travel up and down,
The cream and milk you buy of
me
Is best in all the town.
For custards, puddings, or for tea,
There's none like those you
buy of me.

Oranges.

Here's oranges nice!
At a very small price,
I sell them all two for a penny.
Ripe, juicy, and sweet,
Just fit for to eat,
So customers buy a good many.

Crumpling Codlings.

Come, buy my Crumpling Cod-
lings,
Buy all my Crumplings.
Some of them you may eat raw,
Of the rest make dumplings,
Or pies, or puddings, which you
please.

Old Cloathes to sell, or change for Earthen-ware,
Do you want any damsons or Burgume Pare,
Buy my Oranges or Lemmons.
With dainty Ropes of Oinions,
Come buy my Sweet Williams,
Have you got any Kitchen stuff, Maids?

Four pair for a shilling, Holland Socks,
Your knives for to Grind, buy my ripe Apricocks
Here's to your sharp Vinegar, three pence a Quart,
Also new fresh Herrings, heres 8 for a Groat;
Ends of Gold & Silver,
Ribbons or Garters,
Buy my New Well-fleet Oysters,
Old Bellows, old Bellows to mend.

Buy my Cucumbers fit for the Pickle,
Any Cony-skins Maids, be they never so little,
Here's your Ripe Straw berries six pence a pottle,
Any old Chairs to mend, any broken glass bottle,

Curds and Whay,
Will yo've anything to day,
If you must come awa,
A Pot or a Kettle to mend.

Knives or Scissors, Buckles or Caps,
Here's an excellent Way to Kill all your Ratts,
Hot Custards hot, for two pence a piece,
Will you buy any Walnuts, or old rotten Cheese,
Spectacles for your Noses,
Will you buy any Posies,
Of Curnations and Roses,
Do you want any Butter or Eggs?

Old shooes or boots, will you buy any brooms,
Maids, here's your fine brushes to scrub your rooms;
A Cock or a Pullet, a Capon or Hen,
And here's your old Pin Man a coming agen;
My Basket and Voider,
Rare Patches and Powder,
Come buy my sweet Flounder,
From Holland here's a new Express.

Young Lambs to Sell.

Strawberries.

Get ready your money and come to me,
I sell a young lamb for a penny.
Young lambs to sell! young lambs to sell!
If I'd as much money as I could tell,
I never would cry young lambs to sell.

Rare ripe strawberries and Hautboys, sixpence a pottle.
Full to the bottom, hautboys.
Strawberries and Cream are charming and sweet,
Mix them and try how delightful they eat.

Hot Cross Buns,
One a penny, Buns,
Two a penny, Buns,
Hot Cross Buns.

Here's your toys, for girls and boys,
Only a penny, or a dirty phial or bottle.

LONDON :
Printed by J. Catnach, 2, Monmouth Court, 7 Dials.

Ripe Kentish Cherries for three pence a Pound,
Figg, Figg it away, for I tell you they'r sound,
Hot Pudding Pies, here's two for a Pennie,
Come buy my card Matches, as long as I've anie:
Flowers for your Gardens,
Come buy my bak'd Wardens,
Heres two for a Farthing,
Will you buy my Furbeloe Pears?

Hot Spice Ginger-bread, Taffety Tarts,
Heres a dram of the bottle, to Comfort your hearts.
Dainty fine Ink, you'll lik't when you see't,
Here very good Trotters, with tripe and Neetsfeet,
Come, come away Sir,
Buy a pen Knife or a Razor,
While I am at Leasure;
Have you got any Lanthorns to mend?

Buy a sheet Almanack, hot Grey Pease,
Come, see what you lack, and buy what you please:
A brush for your Shooes, and combs for your hair;
Heres diddle, diddle, diddle dumplings, & Ladies fine Ware,
Old Rags for money,
If you've never so many,
I'll buy more than any;
Heres Milk for a pennie a Quart.

Even such a long list is necessarily selective, and among the many missing trades there is that of the Dog's-meat Man:

THE DOGS'-MEAT MAN.

Every morning when he went by,
Whether the weather was wet or dry,

81

> And right opposite her door he'd stand,
> And cry 'dog's-meat', did this dog's-meat man.
> Then her cat would run out to the dog's-meat man,
> And rub against the barrow of the dog's-meat man,
> And right opposite to her door he'd stand,
> And cry 'Dog's Meat', did this dog's-meat man.

Some callings had more than their fair shaire of resentment: the astonishing outburst in the interpretation of dreaming of chapels (see page 132) is some indication of how the gentlemen of the cloth could be viewed. But this is nothing compared to the vehemence displayed against the Jesuits, as in 'The Popish Priests Complaint at their being forc'd to leave England':

> And is it come to *this*? Are all our *Tricks*
> Prov'd but *Achitophells* vain Politicks?
> Has *Jesuits Powder* lost its force? No Spell
> Or Charm yet left against this *Israel*?
> Loaded with *Vows* and Blessings from the Schools,
> Did we Cross Seas to be both *Knaves* and *Fools*?
> Have we not try'd a thousand ways to scrue
> Our looser *Doctrines* on the sensual Crew?
> Prov'd *Whoredome* Venial, shew'd *Indulgences*,
> And how in *Purgatory* to get Ease,
> Tempted the *Poor* and *Covetous* with Gold
> And oft times Heav'n full cheap to *Fellons* sold,
> Comply'd with *Faction*, allow'd ev'ry Sin,
> To *Slur* Catholick Cause more easie in.

Nor was this attitude confined to any one continent or to any one religion. Samuel Gorton (1592–1677) was a religious radical who was banned in Massachusetts and removed to Rhode Island. Here he was similarly unsuccessful, but he finally settled in Warwick, R.I., where he gathered about him a group called the Gortonites. Among his tenets was disapproval of a paid clergy. The following broadsheet, probably written by one of his followers, shows on what fertile ground his ideas had fallen:

Mr. Samuel Gorton's
Ghost:

or,

The Spirit of PERSECUTION *reprefented in the Similitude of a* DREAM.

> As I lay fleeping on my Bed,
> I dream'd of *Gorton* that is dead,
> Who perfecuted was of old,
> For the Opinion he did hold.

I thought he did riſe up and ſpeak
Concerning thoſe who much do ſeek
For to come in and ſpoil your Peace;
Pray God, *ſaith he*, they don't increaſe,

Or ever Foot-hold get in here,
To ſell the Goſpel by the Year,
And ſeeing they Licenſe have from Heaven
To ſell to you what Christ hath given.

Of *Judas* you may think of old,
Who his bleſt Lord and Maſter ſold
For Silver Pieces Three Times Ten:
So do theſe blind and ſilly Men

Think what they do is very well,
When they the holy Goſpel ſell.
But which is worſt, to ſell the SON,
Or the bleſt Work which he hath done.

Nor did the lawyers fare any better—references to the cunning and extortionate propensities of advocates are commonplace, as in 'The Town in a Hurry':

Misled by a lawyer, who guided the strings

where the corruption is taken for granted as a state of affairs generally and cynically recognized. Again, in 'City Sketches' there is the familiar portrait of the lawyer in the service of local government:

Their chief attendant should be—*mark*—
Their pettifogging wily clerk,
As he, they said had been the cause
Of introducing such d——d laws.

Catnach's 'A Political Alphabet, for the Rise and Instruction of Juvenile Politicians' gives a later indication of the lasting resentment of any interference with the liberty of the people:

K is Fitz. Kelly, such a chap for to jaw,
And can tell you about L A W law;
To get into Cambridge he strove very hard,
Where they sell out fresh butter at 9d. a yard.

But with the abuse, there was also a good-humoured attitude of tolerant contempt, as in the following which occurs occasionally as a fill-up in the chapbooks:

The Lawyer and the Chimney-Sweeper

A rouguish old lawyer was planning new sin,
    As he lay on his bed in a fit of the gout;
The maids and the daylight were just coming in,
    The milkmaids and rush-lights were just going out;

When a chimney-sweep's boy, who had made a mistake,
    Came flop down the flue with a clattering rush,
And bawl'd, as he gave his black muzzle a shake,
    'My master's a-coming to give you a brush.'

'If that be the case,' said the cunning old elf,
    'There's no time to lose—it is high time to flee,—
Ere he gives me a brush, I will brush off myself—
    If I wait for the devil—the devil take me!'

So he limp'd to the door without saying his prayers;
    But Old Nick was too deep to be nick'd of his prey;
For the knave broke his neck by a tumble down stairs,
    And thus ran to the devil by running away.

The following poem is much more good-natured than the eighteenth-century satire that had such a wide circulation wherever there was a drinking party, for the general tenor of the song was known to most people, and the rest could be improvised:

The Lawer's* Pedigree

TUNE – *Our Polly is a ſad Slut.*

A Beggar had a Beadle,
    A Beadle had a Yeoman;
A Yeoman had a prentice,
    A prentice had a Freeman:
The Freeman had a Maſter,
    The Maſter had a Leaſe;
The Leaſe made him a Gentleman,
    And Juſtice of the peace.
The Juſtice being rich,
    And gallant in Deſire,
He marry'd with a Lady,
    And ſo he had a Squire:
The Spuire [*sic*] had a Knight
    Of Courage bold and ſtout;

* *Sic.*

The Knight he had a Lord,
And ſo it came about.

The Lord he had an Earl;
 His Country he forſook,
He travel'd into Spain,
 And there he had a Duke:
The Duke he had a prince,
 The prince a King of Hope
The King he had an Emperor
 The Emperor a Pope.
The Pope he had a Friar,
 The Friar had a Nun:
The Nun ſhe was with Child
 And ſo her Credit ſunk
The Father was a Friar,
 The Iſſue was a Monk.
The Monk he had a Son,
 With whom he did inhabit,
Who when the Father died,
 The Son became Lord Abbot:
Lord Abbot had a Maid,
 And Catch'd her in the Dark,
And ſomething did to her,
 And ſo he had a Clerk.
The Clerk he had a Sexton,
 The Sexton had a Digger;
The Digger had a Prebend,
 The Prebend had a Vicar;
The Vicar had an Attorney,
 The which he took in Snuff;
The Attorney had a Barriſter,
 The Barriſter a Ruff.
The Ruff did get good Counſel,
 Good Counſel get a Fee,
the Fee did get a Motion
 That it might Pleaded be:
the Motion got a Judgment,
 And ſo it came to paſs,
A Beggar's Brat, a ſcolding Knave,
 A crafty Lawyer was.

Boxers, on the other hand, enjoyed universal adulation, and, for example, when a pugilist such as Jack Randall died, the publication of 'A Fancy Elegy' was inevitable:

Alas! poor Jack lies on his back,
    As flat as any flounder:
Although he died of a *bad inside*,
    No *heart* was ever *sounder*.

The *Hole-in-the-Wall* was once his *stall*,
    His *crib* the *Fancy* name it:
A hole in the ground he now has found,
    And no one else will claim it.

But too much *lush* man's strength will crush,
    And so found poor Jack Randall:
His fame once bright as morning light,
    Now's out, like *farthing candle*.

      *   *   *

Good bye, brave Jack!—if each thy track
    Would follow—barring drinking—
What a *noble race* would our country grace
    Firm, *loyal*, and *unshrinking*.

In America, for a very long period, there was a charming custom of
issuing a newsboy's address at the turn of the year, in which he solicited
a present for his services in delivering the newspaper, whatever the
weather:

To the Readers of the South-Carolina and American General Gazette

January 1, 1768.

Throughout the long year paſt, in good or in bad weather,
To wait upon you duly I ſpared nor time nor ſole-leather;
With every bit of news I could either rap or rend,
Hoping to make every reader a good friend;
And if my endeavours have met your approbation,
None happier can be, in any land or nation,

Than I your own News-Boy, no *Mercury* nor *Nuncius*,
For thefe are mere heathen names as you yourfelves are confcious;
My Verfes, true, are lame, but the firft I ever tried,
And the Verfe-men were engaged whenever I applied;
Their founding loud Heroicks, fhort ambling Hudibraftick,
If you look kindly on me, I'll value not of a ftick.
　　Accept a ftave or two, I borrow'd, with my wifhes fervent,
For your health & profperity, from your truly humble fervant,

NATHAN-B. CHILD

Let Virgil's fongs immortalize his name,
And Horace never-fading laurels claim;
Let bards, like thefe, with nobler themes engage,
And emulative wits adorn the age;
My humbler mufe, unpractis'd thus to fing,
Enervate ftrains and harfher notes doth bring;
Yet pardon Sirs, and condefcend to hear,
Your News-Boy's wifhes for a happy year:
May peace and plenty ftill attend your board
And all you give be feventy-fold reftor'd.

This practice was very widespread and, indeed, a whole book could be compiled on this form of broadsheet. The presentation of these addresses varied widely from the simple broadsheet printed on one side, to elaborate four-page folders—sometimes, in their decoration, resembling Valentines, —which might include other poems or at least a calendar for the coming year. The following is one of the simplest:

A

New-Year's-Lay
Dedicated
to the Patrons
of
Liberty Hall and Cincinnati Gazette
January First
1817

ADDRESS

Ye who have cash,—and hearts to give it too—
Receive this artless tributary Lay:
With *gentle eye* the MINSTREL's faults review
And with a *generous hand* the BEARER pay!—

Then will he, gaily dancing on his way,
    With pleasure all his former toils renew;
And wish you many a *happy New-Year's-Day*,
    With grateful bosom, 'loyal, good and true';—
And trust his patrons kind their bounty ne'er will rue.

              THE NEWS-BOY

but the brevity of this poem is no more than the preference of a particular editor, for the following is only part of a very much more elaborate pamphlet:

Montana Post

Carrier's 1869 Annual Address—Our Greeting

Again mid-winter shrouds the plain
    And rends with angry blasts the sky—
A New Year rolls around again,
    Another Year has glided by.

And custom e'er since types were cast
    Demands from me in empty rhymes
Congratulations for the Past,
    And hints and hopes for Future times.

But first just give a thought, my friends,
    To what I've done—and still must do,
Through storm or shine, as heaven sends,
    To furnish latest news to you;

By ev'ry door, through mud and snow,
    I pass ere morn is gray,
And while you dream I onward go
    Upon my dark and dreary way.

Now draw your purses, freely weigh,
    Or 'throw in sight' a good G.B.;*
My time is brief—I can't delay
    To balance scales or change a V.†

* 'bring into view' a 'greenback'.   † five-dollar note.

7. Royalty

May the Queen live for ever!
The glory, the pride of our land!

The seventeenth and eighteenth centuries had seen a never-ending stream
of lampoons, cartoons, squibs, and satirical doggerel that had very little
mercy on the royal family, the church, the government, or any part of
public life that might interfere in the British pursuit of independent
gain. The question of ultimate loyalties had hardly been tested for many
years when the French Revolution provided an unparalleled opportunity.
The result was a flood of loyal statements, of which the following is a
fair example:

Church and King

TUNE – '*Rule, Britannia*'

While o'er the bleeding corpse of France,
    Wild anarchy exulting stands;
And female fiends around her dance,
    With fatal *lamp-cords* in their hands.
CHORUS.—*We Loyal Britons still united sing,*
    Old England's Glory, Church and King.

True Freedom is a temp'rate treat,
    Not savage mirth, nor frantic noise;
'Tis the brisk pulse's vital heat,
    But not a fever that destroys.
CHORUS.—*Let Loyal Britons then unite and sing, &c.*

The Gallic lillies droop and die,
    Profan'd by many a *patriot knave,*
Her Clubs command, her Nobles fly,
    Her Church a Martyr—King a Slave.
CHORUS.—*While Loyal Britons still united sing, &c.*

Yet *Priestly,* Faction's darling child,
    Enjoys this sanguinary scene;
And celebrates with transports wild,
    The *Wrongs,* miscall'd the *Rights,* of men.
CHORUS.—*But Loyal Britons still united sing, &c.*

Whilst pillow'd on his people's breast,
    Our Sovereign sleeps secure, serene;
Unhappy *Louis* knows no rest,
    But mourns his more unhappy Queen.
CHORUS.—*Let Loyal Britons then united sing, &c.*

He finds his *Palace* a *Bastile,*
    Amidst the shouts of Liberty;
Doom'd every heart-felt pang to feel,
    For merely striving to be free.
CHORUS.—*Let Loyal Britons then united sing, &c.*

Go democratic Daemons, go,
    In France your horrid banquet keep!
Feast on degraded *Prelates'* Woe,
    And drink the tears that Monarchs weep.
CHORUS.—*While Loyal Britons still united sing, &c.*

Our Church is built on Truth's firm Rock,
    And mocks each sacrilegious hand;
In spite of each *electric shock,*
    The heav'n-defended steeples stand.
CHORUS.—*While Loyal Britons true united sing, &c.*

Old British sense and British fire,
    Shall guard that Freedom we possess;
Priestly may write, and *Paine* conspire,
    We wish no more and fear no less.
CHORUS.—*While Loyal Britons still united sing,*
    Old England's glory, Church and King.

Politics were never far away, as the references to Priestley and Paine make quite clear. This feeling of the necessity to close ranks against dangerous opinions is more explicit in the broadsheets issued by the Constitutional Society:

The Loyal Briton

Let wicked *Paineites* rail 'gainst Kings,
    'Gainst Government and Laws,
Ne'er heed such base malicious Things,
    Nor e'er espouse their Cause;
But strive their wicked Schemes to foil,
    Their plans to circumvent,
Detect them in their wily Toil,
    And urge them to repent.
             Let us be Loyal to our KING,
                Obedient to the Laws,
             And Heaven, with Influence benign,
                Will aid the glorious Cause.

Mark how with sly envenom'd Tongue,
    They do assail our Ears,
That every Government is wrong,
    Unless 'tis plann'd like theirs:
With Rights of Man, Equality,
    Th'Ignorant they ensnare,
But we'll be virtuous, just, and free,
    Nor in such Rancour share.
             And still be Loyal to our KING, &c.

While Doctrines they throughout the Realm,
    Disperse with knavish Skill,
Weak Minds with Doubts to overwhelm,
    And Democratic Ill;
They'd with Sedition's baneful Train,
    Rush forward like a Flood,
Their wicked Projects to maintain,
    And spill the Royal Blood.
             But we'll be Loyal to our KING, &c.

Then faithful Britons, let's unite
    Against this Russian Band,
'Till Anarchy be banish'd quite
    From this our happy Land:
Then with refulgent Beams of Joy,
    Each honest Heart shall glow,
Celestial Charms which ne'er can cloy,
    We then shall feel below.
             For we'll be Loyal to our KING,
                Obedient to the Laws,
             And Heaven, with Influence benign,
                Will aid the glorious Cause.

The British public always had a lively interest in the members of their royal family, and have had a surprising facility for keeping in touch with even the smallest details of their private lives. 'Farmer George' had wide popularity:

> Hark! from the Trump of Fame,
> Great GEORGE, that much lov'd Name

and his granddaughter, the Princess Charlotte, was even more beloved. The public knew her to be a spirited girl who was not afraid to brook her father's anger in breaking off her engagement to Prince William of Orange. The romance of her marriage to Prince Leopold of Saxe-Coburg appealed very much to the people, and her death a year later in childbirth was the occasion of genuine national mourning:

> She is gone! sweet Charlotte's gone!
> Gone to the silent bourne!
> She is gone, she's gone, for evermore,—
> She never can return.

> She is gone with her joy—her darling Boy,
> The son of Leopold blythe and keen;
> She Died the sixth of November,
> Eighteen hundred and seventeen.

The banality of these lines is explained by the fact that they were of Catnach's own composition!

Loyalty to the Throne was not entirely undiscriminating. Princess Charlotte's mother, Caroline, had long been separated from her husband—George's treatment of her excited quite a lot of sympathy. On his accession, George offered her an annuity of £50,000 to live abroad and renounce the title of Queen:

> And so they sent a MESSENGER,
> To meet the Queen halfway;
> And give her FIFTY THOUSAND POUNDS
> If she abroad would stay;
> And never more be call'd a Queen,
> Or any such a thing,
> But leave them with their dainty dish
> To set before the King.

Caroline rejected this shabby treatment, but the Government instituted proceedings against her for adultery. Although the Divorce Bill was eventually dropped, George had his revenge by causing her to be turned away from the doors of Westminster Abbey on the occasion of his coronation of 19th July 1821. Caroline died four weeks later. 'The Injured Queen of England' was the immediate subject of numerous indignant broadsheets:

> Curs'd be the hour when on the British shore,
> She set her foot—whose loss we now deplore;
> For, from that hour she pass'd a life of woe,
> And underwent what few could undergo:
> And lest she should a tranquil hour know,
> Against her peace was struck a deadly blow;
> A separation hardly to be borne,
> Her only daughter from her arms was torn!
> And next discarded—driven from her home,
> An unprotected Wanderer to roam!
> Oh, how each heart with indignation fills,
> When memory glances o'er the train of ills,
> Which through her travels followed every where
> In quick succession till this fatal year!
> Here let us stop—for mem'ry serves too well,
> To bear the woes which Caroline befel,
> Each art was tried—at last to crush her down,
> The Queen of England was refus'd a crown!
> Too much to bear—thus robb'd of all her state
> She fell a victim to their hate!
> 'They have destroy'd me,'—with her parting breath,
> She died—and calmly yielded unto death.
> Forgiving all, she parted with this life,
> A Queen, and no Queen—wife, and not a wife!
> To Heaven her soul is borne on Seraph's wings,
> To wait the Judgment of the KING of Kings;
> Trusting to find a better world than this,
> And meet her Daughter in the realms of bliss.

With the accession of the Sailor King, British affection for the royal family again declared itself. There is a very amusing and rare broadsheet about an 'apothecary' called Sam Stram, of North Tawton, two of whose children followed in his footsteps. The poem describes how they made names for themselves by diagnosing everything as gastro-enteritis and, regardless of what happened to their patients, continued to treat everyone for this disease. At last the younger Sam comes to the royal notice:

> By these means young Sam Stram's name
> Was carried on the stream of fame,

That reach'd the ears of Royal King Will,
Who having recollected still
The pleasure he had once enjoyed,
When on the seas he was employed,
From reading that amusing tale
Wherein Sangrado ne'er did fail
From the land disease to banish.
Which rais'd his name amongst the Spanish;
And seeing that our hero, Sam,
Practiced just as this very man,
And thinking that he ought to be
Physician to his Majesty,
He was the other day gazetted
King's Physician—Baronetted:
So now our younger Master Sam
In future's call'd Sir Samuel Stram!

In spite of his early liaison with the Irish actress Dorothea Jordan—who bore him ten children—William IV was popular with his people, for he had that bluff, straightforward personality that typified the British concept of their seamen. King Billy received as warm a welcome to the throne as anyone could possibly desire:

Our King is a True British Sailor

Too long out of sight have been kept Jolly Tars,
    In the ground-tiers, like huts stow'd away,
Despis'd and contemn'd were their honour'd scars,
    And Red Coats were Lords of the day.
But Britannia now moves as a gallant first-rate,
    And with transports the Blue Jackets hail her;
For William's right hand steers the helm of the State,
    And our King is a true British Sailor.

No danger the heart of a seaman appals,
    To fight or to fall he is ready,
The safeguard of Britain is her wooden walls,
    And the Helmsman cries, 'Steady! boys, steady!'
Cheer up, my brave boys, give the wheel a new spoke,
    If a foe is in view we will hail her,
For William the Fourth is a sound heart of oak,
    True Blue, and a bold British Sailor.

The attack on the King two years after his accession was therefore bitterly resented. A one-legged seaman threw a stone at William at Ascot and hit him on the forehead. William lived through five more eventful years, which saw the passing of the first Reform Act, the abolition of slavery in the colonies, and the reform of the Poor Laws; and his death was universally lamented:

> When William, the Sailor, belov'd by us all,
>> Was brought to his moorings by death;
> Then ensigns of Britain were struck one and all,
>> And a nation sigh'd o'er his last breath.

It was his successor, however, and her consort and their children, who were the subject of more ballads and broadsheets than all their predecessors. The accession of Victoria was hailed with genuine warmth, and the tributes that followed were innumerable. One of the most amusing is the following:

From the LORD MAYOR: Sir John Cowan, Wax Chandler to Her Majesty

> *Wick*toria, all hail! may thy bonny blue eye
>> Ne'er with tears of dull sorrow be *dripping*,
> May the *stores* all increase, and thy country's *mould*
>> For ever in riches be *dipping*.

> May you never *wax* warm in debate, my dear Queen,
>> Nor care a *rush-light* for the faction;
> For they who'd oppose thy wise councils, I ween,
>> Are *taper* in thought and in action.

Up to his accession, William had been a Whig; but he then turned Tory. Victoria's accession was seen as a complete reversal of the situation in the poem 'The Downfall of the Tories':

> We have got a young and blooming queen,
> As pretty a lass as ever was seen,
> She bawl'd aloud in the royal group,
> Give all the tories a ticket for soup.

This was perhaps as much wishful-thinking as what the Queen is made to say in 'Mr. Ferguson and Queen Victoria':

> And when I open Parliament,
>> Then you'll find I'll do enough,
> I'll take the duty off the tea,
>> Tobacco, gin, and snuff.

I'll make some alterations,
    I'll gain the people's right,
I will have a Radical Parliament,
    Or, they don't lodge here to-night.

I must tell both Whigs and Tories,
    Their tricks I do not fear,
Their sayings all are very fine,
    But they don't lodge here.

About the Whigs and Tories,
    There has been a pretty bother,
I think I'll give the Devil one
    To run away with the other.

From the time of her accession, Queen Victoria never lacked broadside comments on her activities both public and private. Her falling in love with Prince Albert of Saxe-Coburg was a godsend to the ballad-makers and, in many of their contributions, there is a certain amount of wry humour, though sometimes of a rather crude nature:

In the council there the Keveen did swear,
    'Prince Hal, my German cousin—
Stop, Mel.* I pray—you're much too grey,
    I'd choose out of fifty dozen.
It don't suit me to *singular* be,
    These cold nights lying alone, sirs,
Pray, where's my fan? In short, he's the man
    To share Victoria's throne, sirs!'

Och, may be all Ireland won't rejoice,
    The day our Queen is married,
And many a lass will tipple the glass,
    And say—'Too long I've tarried,'
The day she weds, faith! nuptial beds
    Will swarm in exuberance glorious!
The hint they will take, and loyally make
    Young Alberts and Victorias!

But the public had its eye on the public purse: it was generally realized that the expenses of the royal household were probably going to be fairly heavy, as is hinted in the chorus to 'The Queen of the Nice Little Islands':

* Melbourne.

> Don't ax 'em, tax 'em, merrily be,
> Sausages and skillygolee,
> Won't Prince Albert have a spree,
>   When he marries the Queen of England?

A point which Prince Albert is made to confirm in 'The Trubles [*sic*] of a Married Man':

> I am a Foreigner so bold,
>   No Prince was ever riper,
> Me and my wife will dance,
>   And you must pay the Piper.

Catnach and his rivals found plenty to write about: the 'Boy Jones' created a sensation by getting into the Palace; a madman fired twice at the Queen as she and Prince Albert drove up Constitution Hill; and then there was the first baby, the Princess Royal (later, the Crown Princess of Prussia):

> John Bull must handsomely come down
>   With something every year,
> And he may truly to the child
>   Say, 'You're *a little dear.*'
> Sad thoughts will fill his breast whene'er
>   He hears the infant rave,
> Because when hearing a *wight squall*
>   It brings *a notion grave*!
>
> Howe'er, let's give the Princess joy,
>   Though now's her happiest lot;
> For sorrow tends a *palace* more
>   Than e'er it does a *cot*!
> If in some years a son appears,
>   Her claim to rule were vain,
> And being near the *Court* she'll have
>   To *stand out of the* REIGN!

Queen Victoria had four sons and five daughters, and each time there was a new baby the ballad-mongers emphasized anew the increasing cost to the taxpayer, as in this comment on the birth of the Duke of York in '*Another* Present for Old John Bull':

> Oh crikey heres a glorious pull,
>   Another heat for old John Bull,

> In baskets full they'll come oh, lawk,
>> Have you see the Little Duke of York,
>
> He is come to town so gay and mellow,
>> Such a funny little fellow,
> Born without a shirt or Briches
>> Mammy's nose and daddy's breeches.
>
> *   *   *
>
> While Vic and all looks gay and glad,
>> Poor old John Bull seems very sad,
> And cries oh dear what love and joys
>> Lots of little girls and boys.

Nor did the public ever let the Queen forget that she had married a German. Prince Albert's speech was ridiculed, and his austere ideas did not always meet with approval. The following occurs in 'Will you Take the Pledge?':

> Prince albert unto the Queen did say,
>> My dear you go wid me to day, and take de pledge,
> Why albert she says you are mad or drunk
>> May the devil take you, the pledge and the pump.

At this time the humorist Douglas Jerrold (1803–57) was publishing a series of highly successful satires called *Mrs. Caudle's Curtain Lectures*. In these the unfortunate henpecked Caudle is treated each night to a non-stop grumble from his eloquent wife. In themselves they are a brilliant commentary on the life and events of those days. The opportunity was not to be lost: inevitably, a broadsheet appeared, called 'Victoria's Caudle Lectures'. The following refers to the Prince Consort's proposed visit to Germany:

> when you came from Germany you had not got as much as would bait a mouse-trap. I made a gentleman of you, put clothes on your back, and money in your pockets and now you have the impudence to ask for more pocket-money. You help to keep the children? Well, I am sure. You may help to get them Al., and that is all you care about the matter; and now you have the impudence to ask for money. . . .
>
> Why, as for going to Germany Al., I have no great objection, but I must inform you that I have little presents to make to your ragged relations. . . .
>
> I'll tell you what it is Al., you have got too fat, and too saucy since you have resided at the Crown Inn.

It was, however, the Irish who triumphed in the difficult task of reducing the lives of kings and queens to a level that could be understood by the ordinary people:

Looey Philip and Her Grayshus Majesty

—My dear Vic, ses he,
I'm mighty sick, ses he,
For I've cut my stick, ses he,
Tarnation quick, ses he,
From the devil's breeze, ses he,
At the Toolerees, ses he,
For the blackguards made, ses he,
A barricade, ses he—
They're up to the trade, ses he,
An' I was afraid, ses he,
I'd lose my head, ses he,
An' if I lost that, ses he,
I'd have no place for my hat, ses he.

Stop a while, ses she,
Take off your tile, ses she,
You've come a peg down, ses she,
By losin' your crown, ses she.

Mille pardon, ses he,
For lavin' it on, ses he,
But my head isn't right, ses he,
Since I took to flight, ses he,
For the way was long, ses he,
An' I'm not over sthrong, ses he.

Indeed my old buck, ses she,
You look mighty shuck, ses she.

You may say I am, ses he,
I'm not worth a d—n, ses he,
Till I've got a dhram, ses he,
An a cut o' mate, ses he,
For I'm dead bate, ses he,
I'm as cold as ice, ses he.

Oh! never say it twice, ses she,
I'll get you a slice, ses she,
Of sumthin' nice, ses she,
An' will make up a bed, ses she,
In the room overhead, ses she.

I like a matthrass, ses he,
Or a pallyass, ses he,
But in my present pass, ses he,
Anythin' o' the kind, ses he,
I shouldn't much mind, ses he.

8. Children

Little Boys and Girls will find
At Catnach's something to their mind

The need for children to learn their ABC is graphically illustrated not only in the hornbooks with their inscribed pieces of horn attached to wooden blocks with handles, but also in such less clumsy items as *The Royal Battledore* which were current in the eighteenth century. *The Royal Battledore* comprised a piece of thin yellow card, printed on one side, which could be folded in half to fit in the pocket. On the left-hand side there was printed the ABC and some simple combinations of two consonants, beneath which were two short prayers and the Lord's Prayer, with the longer words syllabized. On the right hand there was a series of woodcuts, each representing a letter of the alphabet and illustrated by a suitable and recognizable object—usually an animal. Some letters were difficult to represent: 'Xerxes' stood for X; 'Young Lamb' for Y; and 'Zani' for Z! In the margin were the words:

> He that learns these Letters fair,
> Shall have a Coach to take the Air.

In another leaflet, *The Royal Primer*, issued about the same time, the whole poem, of which only the first two lines appeared in *The Royal Battledore*, is given:

> He who ne'er learns his A, B, C,
> For ever will a Blockhead be;
> But he who to his Book's inclin'd,
> Will soon a golden Treasure find.
>
> Children, like tender Oziers, take the Bow,
> And as the first are fashioned always grow;
> For what we learn in Youth, to that alone,
> In Age we are by second Nature prone.

For those who showed the slightest inclination to heed such advice, the outlook was certainly attractive. Unlike the pamphlets provided for their elders, the children's booklets had as much illustration as text, and many of the woodcuts show signs of great imagination and originality. Some of the American chapbooks of the latter half of the eighteenth century are good examples of this strange mixture of entertainment, moralizing, and pictorializing. Isaiah Thomas, the founder of the American Antiquarian Society, produced many such items, including *Tom Thumb's Play-Book*, which was designed to teach children their letters as soon as they could speak, 'being a New and pleaſant Method to allure LITTLE ONES in the firſt Principles of LEARNING'. This was printed by Isaiah Thomas at Boston in 1762, at the time when he was apprenticed to A. Barclay in Cornhill (Boston). A later product of his, printed and sold at his bookstore in Worcester, Massachusetts, in 1794, was called *Mother Goose's Melody; or, Sonnets for the Cradle*. This contained 'the most celebrated Songs and Lullabies of the good old Nurses, calculated to amuse children and to excite them to sleep'. The second part was devoted to excerpts from Shakespeare, and the whole was 'embellished with cuts, and illustrated with notes and maxims, historical, philosophical, and critical'.

Another of Thomas's productions, *The History of Little Goody Two-shoes; otherwise called Mrs. Margery Twoshoes. With the means by which she acquired her learning and wisdom, and in Consequence thereof her estate*, was 'set forth at large for the Benefit of those,

> Who from a State of Rags and Care,
> And having Shoes but half a Pair,
> Their Fortune and their Fame would fix,
> And gallop in their Coach and six.'

The title-page goes on to advise the reader to 'see the original manuscript in the Vatican at Rome; and the cuts by Michael Angelo; illustrated with the Comments of our great modern Criticks'. Nor were other language-groups neglected: Ambrosius Henkel, at New-Market in Shenandoah County, Virginia, printed in 1811 *Ein Abend-Gesprach, zwischen drey Knaben, in Nord-Carolina*, which was a very stilted conversation between the three boys concerning intemperance and its evil consequences. Henkel's brother Samuel printed at New-Market in 1816 *An interesting narrative of two pious twin children*: this tells how the twins were stolen by a Jew, sold as slaves to the Turks, and finally delivered from death to their father—to which was added, for good measure, the story of 'Charles Berry; or, The Good Son.'

Some of the stories were more interesting, such as the story of *The Old Man, his Children, and the Bundle of Sticks*, printed by Samuel Etheridge at Charlestown about 1815. The old man, having nothing to leave, was on the point of dying:

> A Good old man, no matter where,
> Whether in York, or Lancaſhire,
> Or on a hill or in a dale,
> It cannot much concern the tale;
> Had children very much like others,
> Compos'd of ſiſters and of brothers;

and demonstrates to his children that the bundle of sticks, powerful as a bundle, has little strength or use when divided into its separate parts:

And thus, my countrymen ſhould you,
And I, and all, be firm and true;
If Chriſtian faith and love combine us,
And ſweet affection's cords entwine us;
We need encourage no dejection,
Secure in the DIVINE PROTECTION.
In proſperous days we'll bleſs our GOD,
And when he ſmites we'll kiſs the rod.

—sentiments somewhat similar to those attributed to George Washington, in the last verse of a broadsheet entitled *The Love of Truth Mark the Boy*:

Papa, I *cannot, will not* tell a lie!
My sharp bright hatchet gave the naughty stroke.
The parent then with love and rapture spoke.
Run to my open arms, my dearest boy,
Your *love of truth* bespeaks a father's joy.
My sudden anger and my grief are shed,
Although my lovely cherry-tree is dead.

A poem which is timeless and has had a lasting appeal is *Old Mother Hubbard and her Wonderful Dog*. James Catnach's version was particularly successful in matching illustrations to the words:

Old Mother Hubbard went to the cupboard
  To get the poor dog a bone;
But when she came there the cupboard was bare,
  And so the poor dog had none.

She went to the baker's to buy him some bread,
  When she came back the dog was dead.
Ah! my poor dog, she cried, oh, what shall I do?
  You were always my pride—none equal to you.

She went to the undertaker's to buy him a coffin
  When she came back, the dog was laughing,
Now how this can be quite puzzles my brain,
  I am much pleased to see you alive once again.

She went to the barber's to buy him a wig,
  When she came back he was dancing a jig.
O, you dear merry grig, how nicely you're prancing;
  Then she held up the wig, and he began dancing.

She went to the sempstress to buy him some linen,
  When she came back the dog was spinning
The reel, when 'twas done, was wove into a shirt,
  Which served to protect him from weather and dirt.

To market she went, to buy him some tripe,
    When she came back he was smoking his pipe.
Why, sure, cried the dame, you'd beat the great Jacko,
    Who before ever saw a dog smoking tobacco?

She went to the alehouse to buy him some beer,
    When she came back he sat on a chair.
Drink hearty, said Dame, there's nothing to pay,
    'Twill banish your sorrow and moisten your clay.

She went to the tailor's to buy him a coat,
    When she came back he was riding the goat.
What, you comical elf, the good dame cried,
    Who would have thought a dog would so ride?

She went to the hatter's to buy him a hat,
    When she came back, he was feeding the cat.
The sight made her stare, as he did it so pat,
    While puss sat on the chair, so she showed him the hat.

She went to the shop to buy him some shoes,
    When she came back he was reading the news.
Sure none would believe (she laughed as she spoke),
    That a dog could be found to drink ale and smoke.

She went to the hosier's, to buy him some hose,
    When she came back he was drest in his clothes.
How now? cries the dame, with a look of surprise,
    To see you thus drest, I scarce credit my eyes.

She went to the fruiterer's to buy him some fruit,
    When she came back he was playing the flute.
Oh, you musical dog, you surely can speak:
    Come sing me a song, then he set up a squeak.

She went to the tavern for white wine and red,
    When she came back he stood on his head.
This is odd, said the dame, for fun you seem bred,
    One would almost believe you'd wine in your head.

The dog he cut capers, and turned out his toes,
    'Twill soon cure the vapours, he such attitude shows,
The dame made a curtsey, the dog made a bow,
    The dame said, Your servant, the dog said Bow wow.

Other favourite chapbooks that always sold well were the collections of well-known nursery rhymes, illustrated with small woodcuts. They appeared under various titles, such as *Nurse Love-Child's New Year's Gift for Little Misses and Masters*, and the wording is sometimes different from that in use today:

Pussy-cat, pussy-cat, where have you been?
I've been up to London, to look at the Queen.
Pussy-cat, pussy-cat, what did you do there!
I frightened a little mouse under the chair.

Tell-Tale tit,
Your tongue shall be slit,
And all the dogs in town
Shall have a little bit.

Life is a jest, and all things show it,
I thought so once, but now I know it.

Johnny Armstrong's kill'd a calf,
Peter Henderson got the half;
Willie Wilkinson got the head,
Ring the bell, the calf is dead.

All of a row,
Bent the bow,
Shot at a pigeon
And killed a crow.

Snail, snail come out of your hole,
Or else I will beat you black as a coal.

Bell horses, Bell horses,
What time of day?
One o'clock, two o'clock,
Three and away.

There was an old woman went up in a basket,
Seventy times as high as the moon;
What she did there I could not but ask it,
For in her hand she carried a broom.
'Old woman, old woman, old woman,' said I,
'Whither, oh whither, oh whither so high?'
'To sweep the cobwebs from the sky,
And I shall be back again, by-and-by.'

Hark! Hark!
The dogs do bark,
Beggars are coming to town,
Some in jags,
Some in rags,
And some in velvet gowns.

I'll tell you a story
About Jack-a-Nory,
And now my story's begun,
I'll tell you another
About Jack and his brother,
And now my story's done.

One, two, three,
I love coffee,
And Billy loves tea.
How good you be,
One, two, three,
I love coffee,
And Billy loves tea.

As I went to Bonner,
I met a pig,
Without a wig,
Upon my word and honour.

See-saw, sacradown,
Which is the way to London town?
One foot up, and the other down,
And that is the way to London town.

Hey diddle, the cat and the fiddle,
The cow jumped over the moon,
The little dog laughed to see the sport,
And the dish ran away with the spoon.

Ding, dong, bell!
Pussy's in the well.
Who put her in?
Little Johnny Green.
Who pulled her out?
Little Johnny Snout.
What a naughty boy was that,
To drown poor pussy cat,
Who never did him any harm,
And kill'd the mice in his father's barn.

Jack and Jill went up the hill,
To get a pail of water;
Jack fell down and broke his crown,
And Jill came tumbling after.

Cock a doodle do,
The dame has lost her shoe,
And master's lost his fiddle stick
And don't know what to do.

I had a little husband,
No bigger than my thumb,
I put him in a quart pot,
And there I bid him drum.

Who's there? A Grenadier!
What do you want? A pot of beer.
Where's your money? Oh, I forgot.
Then get you gone, you drunken sot.

Hush-a-bye, baby, on the tree top;
When the wind blows the cradle will rock.
When the bough breaks the cradle will fall,
Down comes the baby, cradle and all.

There was an old woman that lived in a shoe,
She had so many children she knew not what to do;
She gave them some broth without any bread,
Then she beat them all well, and sent them to bed.

Needles and pins,
Needles and pins;
When a man marries
His trouble begins.

Young lambs to sell,
Young lambs to sell,
If I'd much money as I could tell,
I wouldn't cry young lambs to sell.

Goosey, goosey, gander,
Whither dost thou wander?
Up stairs and down stairs,
And in my lady's chamber;
There you'll find a cup of sack,
And plenty of good ginger.

The lion and the unicorn fighting for the crown,
The lion beat the unicorn round about the town;
Some gave them white bread, some gave them brown,
Some gave them plum cake, and sent them out of town.

> The cock doth crow
> To let you know,
> If you be wise
> 'Tis time to rise.

> My mother and your mother
> Went over the way;
> Said my mother to your mother,
> It's chop-a-nose day!

The children's stories in chapbooks were usually unillustrated, apart from the occasional woodcut on the title-page. *Beauty and the Beast* often lacked even that. But the story was vigorously told: when the merchant picked a rose to take back to his daughter, the Beast was extremely angry. The merchant tried in vain to placate him by explaining his action:

'My name is not My Lord,' replied the monster, 'but Beast. I don't like compliments, not I; I like people to speak as they think; and so do not imagine I am to be moved by any of your flattering speeches, but you say you have daughters. I will forgive you, on condition that one of them come willingly, and suffer for you.'

Jack the Giant Killer was usually graced with a fine portrayal of a giant, one of the many that Jack despatched in the course of his professional life. There is more variety and humour in this story than in most, and the

THE OX TURNED BUTCHER.

THE REWARD OF ROGUERY, OR THE ROASTED COOK.

THE
WORLD
TURNED
UPSIDE DOWN
OR THE
FOLLY OF MAN
EXEMPLIFIED

IN TWELVE COMICAL RELATIONS

UPON

UNCOMMON SUBJECTS

*Illustrated with Twelve curious Cuts
Truly adapted to each Story*

GALLÁNTRY—A LÁ MODE—OR THE LOVERS CATCHED
BY THE BIRD.

THE OLD SOLDIER TURNED NURSE.

PRINTED AND SOLD IN LONDON

THE DUEL OF THE PALFRIES.

SUN, MOON, STARS AND EARTH TRANSPOSED.

THE MAD SQUIRE AND HIS FATAL HUNTING.

THE WATER WONDER, OR FISHES LORDS OF THE CREATION.

---

author was clearly uncertain whether he was writing for adults or children:

> When he [Jack] was no more than seven years of age, his father sent him into the field to look after his oxen. A country Vicar, by chance, one day coming across the field, called Jack, and asked him several questions; in particular, How many commandments were there? Jack told him, there were nine. The Parson replied, there are ten. Nay, quoth Jack, master Parson, you are out of that; it is true that there were ten, but you broke one of them with your own maid Margery. The Parson replied, thou art an arch wag, Jack. Well, master Parson, quoth Jack, you have asked me one question, and I have answered it; let me ask you another. Who made these oxen? the Parson replied, God. You are out again, quoth Jack, for God made them bulls, but my father and his man Hobson made oxen of them.

The story of *Blue Beard*, which has such rich possibilities, is disappointingly done, and so briefly written that only the tales's reputation warrants its being given the title role, instead of the second—and longer—account of an ancient and dismal legend, *The Murder Hole*. For those who found reading difficult, the most satisfying of all the chapbooks was the fascinating *The World turned Upside Down; or The Folly of Man, exemplified in twelve comical relations upon* UNCOMMON SUBJECTS. It is true that there was a rhyming commentary of excessive tediousness, but this could be ignored, since the pictures told their own fascinating story. There was the child beating his father, and the daughter tending her sick mother. In 'The Ox Turned Farmer', the ox whips two farmers into greater effort as they drag the plough across the field. The old soldier is given the baby to tend, while the nurse girds herself with a sword and shoulders a rifle. A hen and a hare turn the spit on which is stretched the unfortunate cook. Two horses joust, mounted upon their masters' backs. The ox acts as butcher to the carcase of his master; the bird catches the lovers in a snare. The ass prods his master as he staggers home under a heavy load; and the horse grooms his master in the stable. Fishes angle for human beings; and the sun, moon and stars are surmounted by the earth. The story was so well known that its name was even given to public houses—a sure sign of its popular appeal.

9. Religious

Here are choicest treasures hid;
Here my best comfort lies.
Isaac Watts

Among the chapman's varied bundle of ballads, stories of crimes and the supernatural, fairy stories, fortune-tellers, and ancient legends, there were always some pamphlets of a more serious nature. Some of these were sermons, while others dealt more directly with the Bible stories and teaching. It is notable that the latter were—unique among chapbooks— remarkable for the number, size, and vigour of their illustrations. The text in fact played a secondary part and the illustrations, like the wall- paintings in medieval churches, helped to explain to old people and children what they could scarcely have read for themselves.

Outstanding among these are the versions of *The Pilgrim's Progress* that sold steadily over many decades. Crude editions of the full text, illustrated with very rough woodcuts, were current throughout the period of the chapbooks but, cheap though they were, they were out of reach of the poorest of the people. Moreover, the chapbooks had the additional attraction of hitting the high-lights in much the same fashion as a modern medley of tunes from an opera will concentrate on just those airs that everyone knows well and likes. Thus Christian, arriving at the gate over which is inscribed:

KNOCK AND IT SHALL BE OPENED

is depicted as being admitted by Goodwill while Beelzebub and his lively devils make a derisive demonstration on their battlements. As Christian lifts up his eyes to the Palace Beautiful, two amiable lions are shown gambolling before him. Far more dramatic is his encounter with Apollion who, portrayed in horrible guise, advances on Christian with unmistakable menace. The mouth of Hell is artistically depicted with a number of heraldic-looking creatures surrounding Christian in the smoke and the flames. In the trial before Mr Hategood, the learned judge is shown in the full and awesome regalia of the English eighteenth-century court, though in the background there is a witness who resembles Caiaphas in his dress. One of the most charming scenes is the meeting of Christian and Faithful with the Shepherds of the Delectable Mountain: here is a true English rural landscape with the dress of the period which survived in remote parts even into the nineteenth century. The meal at the house of the Interpreter shows children seated on stools sharing their elders' repast served in wooden bowls—and the eldest boy is pulling his younger brother's hair. In all, twenty-one large illustrations are accompanied by only some thirteen hundred words of text, so that the very detailed and lively pictures would have a strong attraction for people who could not cope with the usual closely printed chapbook with its single uninformative woodcut on the cover.

Next in favour were the many different versions of the Bible and its more famous stories. *The New Pictorial Bible*, for example, included two small and indifferently printed woodcuts on every page, below each of which it gave the Biblical reference, accompanied by the actual text. Out of forty-seven illustrations, six are devoted to the Creation, and another twenty-three to the rest of the Old Testament. Noah sends his animals two by two into a substantial looking ark; the Tower of Babel comprises concentric circles of arcades tapering off into the sky; Abraham offers Isaac for sacrifice; Joseph is cast into the pit, and is later tempted by Potiphar's Wife; the infant Moses is discovered and later smites the rock, and still later receives the Tables; Samson pulls down the pillars of the Philistine's palace; David kills Goliath; while Solomon's Temple looks remarkably like Burlington House. The scenes from the New Testament are equally predictable, ending with a crowded Last Day scene. Nevertheless, the achievement is remarkable: in twenty-four pages some of the main Bible lessons have been conveyed in a very attractive way, and without any of the hint of condescension which spoilt so many of the tracts of the later nineteenth century.

The inevitable brevity of the chapbook Bibles was overcome by additional pamphlets treating various stories in far greater detail. *The History of Abraham, Isaac, and Jacob* has larger and clearer illustrations and eschews Biblical texts (although chapter and verse are always quoted) in favour of interpretation. The pictures have their own impressive originality, which is matched by the language of the descriptions. Below a fine representation of Jacob and Esau in what appears to be a prosperous eighteenth-century kitchen, there is the explanation:

After the happy consummation of Isaac's marriage with Rebekah, Abraham lived many years, till at length transported to that better and heavenly country; having spent one hundred and seventy-five years in the exercise of holy virtues and graces. God, after his death, multiplied his blessings on Isaac his son. But they had been twenty years married without having any children, when Isaac prayed the Lord for his wife's sake for children, and he was heard, and Rebekah was delivered of male twins. The Divine oracle stated that the elder should serve the younger. When these two children were grown up, Jacob, the youngest, on a time sod [cooked] lentil pottage, and Esau, returning from hunting, extremely hungry, with greediness desired this pottage; which Jacob perceiving, would not part with it till he had promised to sell him his birthright in consideration thereof, to which Esau agreed.

Much more text, most of it—apart from the frequent quotations from the Old Testament—of a prosaic nature, accompanies the fascinating illustrations in *The History of Moses*. The invasion of the frogs in Pharaoh's palace, and the burning of Nadab and Abihu, are particularly well depicted. But it is *The History of Joseph and His Brethren* which makes a break with tradition, and renders the whole story into one lengthy poem. Thus, on the page headed 'Tempted by Potiphar's Wife':

> When Joseph to the land of Egypt came,
> One Potiphar a man of noted fame,
> Bought him with silver and preferred him straight
> Making him steward of his whole estate.
> On whom his mistress cast her wanton eyes,
> And he reproved her, and said be wise,
> And cast, henceforth, these idle thoughts away—
> How can I do that wicked thing, I pray?
> Now finding her entreaties would not do,
> She went to seize him, but away he flew,
> Leaving his garment in her hand also;
> Now from that time she proved his mortal foe:
> She said, my Lord (when he returned at night),
> Thy Hebrew strove with all his might,
> To mock thy lady, but was ne'er her near,
> I cried, he fled, and left his garment here.

—the scene being embellished with a canopied bed, with Potiphar's wife in an extravagant nightdress, and Joseph fleeing from her—his garb resembling closely that of a page from some Renaissance Italian painting.

Side by side with the Biblical stories there were the prayer books, and these—to modern eyes—bring home the true meaning of the words Family Prayers that occur so often in the novels of the eighteenth and nineteenth centuries. Thus the Family Morning Prayer fills more than three pages, the Family Evening Prayer more than two. It is true that there is a helpful notice on the title page:

> . . . all the Prayers are so arranged, that when any one is too long to be used without inconvenience, it may be shortened by leaving out some of the paragraphs; and this may be done without injury to the connection.

—but this could have had some unexpected results. Thus in the prayer For the Due Discharge of Domestic Duties, the servants might have appreciated the omission of the following:

> Teach and incline servants to do their work with singleness of eye, as unto Christ: to be ambitious of serving their masters with all fidelity, and of preventing all just cause of anger or rebuke from them for obstinacy, sloth, or carelessness. Grant them wisdom to consider their station not

as any hardship, much less any disgrace to them, but as the post which thy fatherly love hath appointed them to fill. Give them to understand to their great peace and strong consolation, that by doing their work from a principle of faith and love to Christ Jesus, they may stand as high in thy favour, and grow as rich towards God, as if their condition entitled them to all respect from the world. And may they never imagine they are religious and Christian altogether, any longer than they abstain from all those frauds and deceits which they are tempted to use for filthy lucre's sake.

On the other hand, they would proably have preferred to retain the counterpart to this passage in the next paragraph:

O! convince the rich that it is not their merit, but thy providence alone that makes the different of station, and appoints the subordination: not that they should be as tyrants in their houses, and imperious to their servants, but that they should add to the comfort of those who are under them. Enable them, therefore, carefully to avoid hurting those who labour for them, by their frowardness and behaving towards them with such rudeness, as they would be ashamed to shew to any equal. Imprint upon their minds a lively remembrance that they have a master in heaven, who is no respecter of the persons of men, before whom both masters and servants must give a strict and solemn account of their behaviour to each other. Inspire all who preside in families not only with justice, but with mercy and piety towards their servants.

One of the strangest of all the chapbooks of this kind is *An Elegy in memory of that valiant champion, Sir R. Grierson, late Laird of Lag, who died Dec. 23d, 1733. Wherein the Prince of Darkness commands many of his best friends, who were the Chief Managers of the late Persecution.* This is an elaborate satire, in which Satan mourns the death of one of his most faithful mortal aides:

What fatal news is this I hear?
On earth who shall my standard bear?
For Lag who was my champion brave,
Is dead and now laid in his grave.

Grierson (c. 1655–1733), a Scottish Jacobite, persecuted the Covenanters with the utmost cruelty, and was one of the judges under whom the Wigtown martyrs suffered. Satan is warm in his praise of his servant's steadfastness, particularly on Sundays which the Laird appears to have reserved for his worst excesses. He says that Cain could never rival Grierson—no more could Doeg the Edomite or Herod or Claverhouse. During the course of this long poem, Satan takes the opportunity to praise the work of others of his disciples such as Charles Stewart, Monmouth, and James II—

> He framed all mischief by a law,
> To make Scotland an aceldama,
> Threatened to make a hunting field
> Of shires that would not fully yield,
> He all the venom of the pit
> Against piety did spit.

The picture painted in this poem of more than 700 lines is one of unremitting savagery as the bitter religious persecutions of the late seventeenth and early eighteenth centuries pursued their inexorable way in a country that could well have been rid of such unscrupulous and self-seeking men as Grierson and the many opportunists of those times. As Satan concludes:

> On earth no more they can serve me,
> But still I have their company.

If family prayers were lengthy, they merely reflected the lengthy church services to which, until the twentieth century, the population was fully accustomed. In a famous church at Whitby can still be seen evidence of the way in which the congregation of the past coped with the problem of spending two or three hours in church. Spacious square pews with individual heating stoves fill the church, and it is clear that whole families settled down in as much comfort as they could muster to sit out the interminable Sunday services of the seventeenth and eighteenth centuries. One of the popular chapbooks of those times was *A Wedding-Ring Fit for the Finger* 'laid open in a sermon preached at a wedding in St. Edmonds by William Secker'. It is difficult to believe nowadays that this 6,000-word sermon was actually delivered in full to a wedding-party anxious to proceed with the next stage in the celebrations, but on the contrary it may well be that the congregation of that time might have considered anything less imposing would have detracted from the importance of the occasion. The sermon is an elaborate and intricately argued exposition of the whole state of marriage, and is notable for the grandeur of language of some of its passages:

> Marriage is the tying of such a knot, that nothing but death can unloose. Common reason suggests so much, that we should be long a-doing that which can but once be done. Where one design hath been graveled in the sands of delay, thousands have been split on the rock of precipitance. Rash adventures yield gain. Opportunities are not like tides, that when one is past, another returns; but yet take heed of flying without your wings; you may breed such agues in your bones, that may shake you to your graves.

The fanciful title of the sermon is typical of the period. Other chapbook titles include *The Plant of Renown, A Choice Drop of Honey from the Rock Christ,* and *Sins and Sorrows Spread before God*—the last two by Thomas Wilcocks and Isaac Watts respectively.

Probably the strangest of all the religious chapbooks, and one that had a very wide circulation, is the mysterious *The Wife of Beith*, which is described as 'an allegorical dialogue, containing nothing but what is recorded in Scripture'. This poem of over 600 lines is a perverse kind of Pilgrim's Progress. It begins:

> In Beith once dwelt a worthy wife,
> Of whom brave Chaucer mention makes
> She lived a licentious life,
> And namely in veneral acts
> But death did come for all her cracks;
> When years were spent and days out driven,
> Then suddenly she sickness takes,
> Deceased forthwith, and went to heaven.

On her way the Wife of Beith meets Judas Iscariot, who assures her that she must pass the gates of Hell if she is to attain Heaven. In a lively conversation with Lucifer he rejoins to her declaration that she would not enter Hell:

> I will not have you here good dame,
> For you were mistress of the flyting,
> If once within this gate you come,
> I will be troubled with your bitings
> Cummer, go back, and let me be,
> Here are too many of your rout,
> For women lewd like unto thee,
> I cannot turn my foot about.

After a long and painful climb the Wife of Beith eventually arrived before the resplendent city of Jerusalem, but the gates were shut and she beat upon them until 'father Adam' answered:

> Who is't that raps so rudely there,
> Heaven cannot well be won by weir.

To her request for admittance Adam says no sinners may come in, but Eve says that she would like to have the company of another woman. However, Eve says she must return later when she is free of crime. The Wife of Beith retorts that her guilt had its origin in Eve's own deceit. Stung by this, Eve complains to Noah, who says he will deal with the situation. Accordingly he confronts the Wife of Beith:

> Go back, he said, ye drunken lown,
> You're none of the celestial flock.

The Wife of Beith, far from being nonplussed, retorts with spirit:

> Noah, she said, hold thy piece [*sic*],
> Where I drank ale, thou didst drink wine,
> Discovered was to thy disgrace,
> When thou wast full like to a swine:
> If I was drunk I learned at thee,
> For thou'rt the father and the first,
> That others taught, and likewise me,
> To drink when as we had no thirst.

The Wife of Beith continues to best her adversaries—Abraham, Jacob Lot, Moses, Aaron, Samson, David, Jonas, and Thomas—until at last she asks for Mary Magdalene:

> Sister, quoth she, give me your hand
> Are we not both of one vocation;
> It is not through your occupation,
> That you are placed so divine,
> My faith is fixed on Christ's passion,
> My soul shall be as safe as thine.

Bur Mary Magdalene is fearful of helping her, and asks Paul to 'put the wife in better tune'. But neither he nor Peter can convince her of her unworthiness, and at last the Lord himself 'environed with angels bright' tells her she must go. Unabashed, the Wife of Beith continues her pleading, drawing example after example from the Gospels to counter his reasoning. In desperation, at last she cries:

St Thaddeus

> Save now, good Lord, my silly soul,
> Bought with thine own most precious blood
> Sweet Lord my God, say me not nay,
> For if I perish here I'll die.

The Lord relents at these words:

> Poor silly wretch, then speak no more,
> Thy faith, poor soul hath saved thee;
> Enter thou into my glore [*sic*],
> And rest thro' all eternity.

This extraordinary poem, in its original conception and its fresh and colourful language, stands head and shoulders above nearly everything else in the chapman's pack, and it is surprising that later ages have ignored its existence for so long.

Judas Iscariot's apocryphal life and death was also the subject of a chapbook, inappropriately adorned with a woodcut depicting an eighteenth-century squire angrily commanding a small boy to come down from a tree where he is hiding. The 'lost and undone sone of perdition' is described as the first born of a tanner of Joppa. His mother dreamt that he would prove both a thief and a murderer and bring her and her generation to shame and disgrace. When Judas was born, he was seen to have under his left breast the marks of a cross, a gallows, two daggers, and several pieces of money. A magician confirmed the truth of the dream, and agreed to have a little boat made in which the child could be safely launched on the Jordan and left to the mercy of providence:

After she was gone, the magician sent for one Rot, a very cunning Artist, a Joiner by trade, who undertook to make the boat, drawing out with his pencil, the form of it, carried it home with him, wrought upon it in private, and having soon finished it, brought it to the magician's house, who paid him largely for it.

The boat was made 'like a shell, with a cover to go down close so that no water might get in, and a little vent to let in air at the top, and room in it to lie soft and easy'. The mother and her kinswoman dressed the child in many warm and rich garments, with an upper coat of oil, so that no water might penetrate it, and they put a notice round his neck:

MY NAME IS JUDAS

The child is borne away to the coast of Iscariot where Pheophilus the king and his nobles discover the beautiful smiling baby. The king treats him as his own child, has him well educated, and makes him his principal steward.

But Judas is ambitious and unscrupulous. He slays the prince in the hope of being made heir to the throne. His conscience, however, overcomes him, and he leaves the kingdom, travelling as a menial. In the course of his wanderings he slays his own father, later—and unwittingly—marries his mother and, when at last the truth is discovered through the marks on his body, resumes his wandering filled with remorse. Eventually he finds Christ and his followers in the land of Judaea, and from this point the story follows the Gospel narrative fairly accurately:

> Tho' Judas 'mongst the Apostles was
> And with them took his part,
> His awful end proved him to be
> A traitor in his heart.

One of the most enjoyable of the offerings in this field is an old Irish ballad:

> Oh! St. Patrick was a gentleman,
> Who came of decent people;
> He built a church in Dublin town,
> And put it on a steeple.
> His father was a Gallagher,
> His mother was a Brady;
> His aunt was an O'Shaughnessy,
> His uncle an O'Grady.
> So, Success attend St. Patrick's fist,
> For he's a saint so clever;
> Oh! he gave the snakes and toads a twist,
> He bothered them for ever!

> The Wicklow hills are very high,
> And so's the Hill of Howth, Sir;

But there's a hill, much bigger still,
 Much higher nor them both, sir.
'Twas on the tope of this high hill
 St. Patrick preached his sarmint,
That drove the frogs into the bogs,
 And banished all the varmint.
  Oh, Success, &c.

There's not a mile in Ireland's isle
 Where dirty varmin musters,
But there he put his dear fore-foot,
 And murdered them in clusters.
The toads went pop, the frogs went hop,
 Slap dash into the water,
And the snakes committed suicide
 To save themselves from slaughter.
  Oh, Success, &c.

Nine hundred thousand reptiles blue
 He charmed them with sweet discourses,
And dined on them at Killaloe
 In soups and second courses.
Where blind worms crawling in the glass
 Disgusted all the nation,
He gave them a rise, which opened their eyes
 To a sense of their situation.
  Oh, Success, &c.

No wonder that those Irish lads
 Should be so gay and frisky,
For sure St. Pat, he taught them that,
 As well as making whisky;

No wonder that the Saint himself
　　Should understand distilling,
Since his mother kept a sheebeen shop
　　In the town of Enniskillen.
　　　　Oh, Success, &c.

Oh! was I but so fortunate
　　As to be back in Munster,
'Tis I'd be bound, that from that ground
　　I never more would once stir.
For there St. Patrick planted turf,
　　And plenty of the praties;
With pigs *galore, ma gra, ma 'store,*
　　And cabbages,—and ladies.
　　　　Then my blessing on St. Patrick's fist,
　　　　　　For he's the darling Saint, O!
　　　　Oh, he gave the snakes and toads a twist,
　　　　　　He's a beauty without paint, O!

Another song, however, casts further light in one of its verses on the
miracle of the banishment of the snakes, and on the drinking habits of
the Irish since that event:

You've heard, I suppose, long ago,
　　How the snakes, in a manner most antic,
He marched to the County Mayo,
　　And trundled them into th'Atlantic.
Hence, not to use water for drink,
　　The people of Ireland determine;
With mighty good reason, I think,
　　Since St. Patrick has filled it with vermin,
　　　　And vipers, and such other stuff!

10. Dreams

Books about fortune-telling and charms have never lacked a public, and they were one of the most popular classes of books carried by the chapmen, particularly in rural districts. The buyers had a wide choice. There were *The Golden Dreamer, The True Fortune Teller, Mother Bunch's Golden Fortune-Teller, The Dreamer's Oracle, Napoleon's Book of Fate,* and several others of less fame. Not every printer was devoid of conscience concerning the profits to be made from this type of publication. At least one nineteenth-century Scottish publisher insisted on printing in small type a warning—like those appearing nowadays on cigarette packets—'To the Reader,' at the end of the booklets he produced:

> The foregoing pages are published principally to show the superstitions which engrossed the mind of the population of Scotland during a past age, and which are happily disappearing before the progress of an enlightened civilization. It is hoped, therefore, that the reader will not attach the slightest importance to the solutions of the dreams as rendered above, as dreams are generally the results of a disordered stomach, or an excited imagination.

—a notice that appeared even on fortune-telling booklets that did not deal with dreams at all! In reading the popular literature of the period, it is of course well to be aware of the significance of dream omens if one is to gain a good understanding of their contents.

The dream books are remarkably detailed and their contents are presented in an imperfect dictionary order. They do not always agree: on the other hand, there are places where the wording indicates that one has copied from the other. In spite of the printer's warning, it seems likely

that the fortune-telling booklets were well used, for very few copies have survived. The main items covered included the following:

Abuse–To dream that you are abused or insulted is a sure sign that you will have a dispute with some person.

A-bed–To dream that you are in bed, betokens good health, but beware, for some one wishes to injure you.

Abroad–If you dream you are in a foreign country, some one who is making money abroad is likely to bequeath a fortune to you.

Actress–To dream of an actress, not performing on the stage, denotes to the lover that careful attention must be paid to all her undertakings and all will be well.–To men of business, it is a sure sign of success.

Acquaintance–To dream you quarrel or fight with an acquaintance, it is an unlucky omen, it forebodes a division among your own family, much to the injury and prejudice of the dreamer.

Adorn–Should you dream of being gaily dressed in splendid apparel, denotes a sure sign of some affliction to yourself or your relatives.–If your dress be in black, it denotes prosperity and good success attending your undertakings.

Adultery–If a man dreams of committing adultery, he must be cautious in his speculations and not be too eager in going a-head in his business. –To a woman, if unmarried, she must remove in the man who is paying his addresses to her all manner of unbecoming speech or behaviour to her, or else it will prove her ruin.–If a married woman, it denotes happiness in her family, and a large offspring.

Agricultural Implements–This is a good dream to either man or woman; it denotes good luck, very fortunate, and plenty to live upon.

Alehouse–To dream of drinking in an alehouse, denotes that you must be careful in your transactions; should you be drunk in the house is a sure omen of bad fortune.

Altar–To dream you are at the altar betokens joy and gladness; if at the Hymeneal altar, the marriage will be deferred.

Alms–To dream that they are begged of you, and you deny to give them, shews want and misery to the dreamer, but to dream that you give them freely, is a sign of joy and long life.

Anchor–To dream you see an anchor, signifies great and certain hope.

Angels–To dream of angels is a sign that someone is near you—the remaining part of your dream will prove true, be therefore mindful of it. If you are in love, nothing can be more favourable, and your undertakings will prosper.

Ye Banks an' Braes.

Anger–To dream that you are angry with any one denotes, that you have many enemies, and that some evil design is formed against your happiness.

Angling–If you are fishing in a clear stream, it is an excellent dream. Should you be fishing in muddy water, you must be aware of those who are pretending great friendship.

Apron–If you dream of your apron falling off, it is a sure sign of good. –If your apron be on and a very rich one, be very cautious of your lover; for if he be not very attentive to you, he will give you the slip—if he is attentive, watch him.

Anthem–To dream of singing an anthem with many others beside you denotes a long journey you will be engaged in, and will arrive safe home and bring plenty with you.

Apparel–To dream that your apparel is proper and suited to the season of the year, denotes prosperity and happiness.

Apples–To dream that you see apple-trees, and eat sweet and ripe apples, denotes joy, pleasure, and recreation, especially to virgins, but sour apples signifies contention and sedition.

Anxiety–To dream that you are anxious to accomplish any project denotes that you will soon tire of it; to think that your mind is anxious or uneasy, is a sign that some one wishes to do you a favour.

Asses–To dream you ride an ass that bears your blows, and the more you beat it the slower his pace, denotes you will be married to a virtuous industrious wife, but your passion will ruin her.–If the ass mends his pace under your blows, and throws you, she will prove inconstant.

Baby–If you dream that you have a baby nursing is a sign of some misfortune. If the baby is sickly, a sure sign of death.

Bacon–To dream you are eating fat bacon, you will have abundance of work to perform that day, and apply yourself to it.

Bakehouse–If you are in a bakehouse where there is plenty of bread, you will have a large increase in your family, and an equal proportion in your business.

Bank–To dream of being in a bank and doing business therein, is a sure sign of success.

Baptize–To dream that someone is baptizing you is a sign of going on a journey.

Barefooted–To dream you are barefooted is a good dream. A law suit will take place in your family, and you will obtain a verdict in your favour with all costs.

Barn–To dream you see a barn well stored with corn, shows that you will marry a rich wife.

Basin–To dream you are eating or drinking out of a basin, is a certain sign that you will soon be in love.

Bathing–To dream you are bathing in clear water is a splendid dream, and a sure sign of good fortune in all your undertakings. If the water be rough and muddy, be careful.

Battle–If you dream of seeing a battle, beware of secret enemies, who will endeavour to hurt you; if you are in love, your sweetheart is false.

Bay-tree–To dream of a bay-tree denotes success in your undertakings.

Beasts–To dream some furious beast pursues you, and you cannot avoid it, betokens your enemies will prevail against you.

Beef–To dream of beef denotes the death of a friend or relation.

Beer–To dream of beer portends accident. Beware! and abstain.

Bees–To dream that you see bees at work signifies that your industry will be successful; if they are flying about, bad reports will be spread of you; if they sting you, you will suffer loss of reputation.

Birds–To dream you hear birds singing is a sign of happiness.–To dream of finding an empty nest denotes losses and great uneasiness.

Cakes–To dream that one makes them, signifies joy and profit; to dream of cakes without cheese is good; but to dream of both, signifies deceit in love.

Candy–To dream you are eating candy denotes you will have a large business in your lifetime and plenty of children.

Cards–To dream that you are playing at cards, denotes that you will soon be in love, if you are not so already.

Cattle–To dream you are keeping cattle denotes disgrace.

Cat–If any dream that he hath encountered a cat, or that he hath killed one, he will commit a thief to prison, and prosecute him to death; for the cat signifies a common thief.

Cell–To dream of you being in a prison cell is a sure sign of going a voyage to sea.

Chambermaid–To dream you are performing the duties of a chambermaid

is a token of good.–If you are in the act of showing a man to bed, your marriage is not far off, and a good husband you will get.–If it be a woman you are showing, it denotes trouble; beware of some one not far from you speaking of you as a friend but a traitor behind your back.–If children with the woman it is still worse.

Chains–To dream that you are in chains shows that you will be unfortunate after marriage; but to dream you have another in chains, success in matrimony.

Chapel–If you see the priest in the chapel, it is a bad omen, you had better dream of old belzebub as the man in the long robes.

Cheese–To dream you eat cheese, denotes profit.

Cherries–To dream of cherries betokens disappointments in life, vexations in marriage, falsehood in love, and deceitful pleasure.

Children–To dream you have children is a sign you will die happy in your family.

Clock–To dream you hear the clock strike shows that you will be speedily married.

Clouds–To dream you are out walking, and you see plenty of bright, beautiful clouds, and the sun shining, is great success in your business.

Coals–To dream of coals is a sign of riches.

Coal-pits–To dream of being at the bottom of coal-pits signifies matching with a widow; for he that marries her must be a continued drudge, and yet shall never find the bottom of her policies.

Coach–To dream of riding in a coach denotes that you will love idleness, and are given to pride.

Combing–For any person to dream of combing his or her own hair is good for both man and woman; for it signifies to get out of evil times or affairs.

Corn–To dream you are gathering ripe corn, denotes success in your enterprise; but if it is blighted or mildewed, you will be a great loser.

Comets–To dream you see comets, is ominous of war, plague, famine, and death.

Courting–To dream of courting a beautiful woman, betokens crosses and vexations.

Cuckoo–To dream you hear the cuckoo, your sweetheart will prove a coquette.

Cupid–To dream cupid breaks his dart, your love will change.–If he breaks his bow you will die an old maid.

Currants–To dream of black currants denotes great happiness in the married state. But if the currants are red, beware of false friends, those whom you little expect, for they will do you harm if they possibly can.

Dancing–To dream you are dancing at a ball foretells you will soon receive some news from a long absent friend.

Deaf–To dream of being deaf or in the company of some one deaf, denotes that you will soon be married and have a steady man.

Death–To dream you see this grim looking bundle of bones, denotes happiness and long life, and you will be either speedily married yourself, or else assist at a wedding.

Debt–To dream you are in debt and pursued by officers, denotes that you will fall into some unexpected difficulties, or great danger.

Deer–To dream you see deer in a park, denotes war and famine; to the lover, it foretells some very unpleasant dispute with your sweetheart.

Demolish–To dream you are destroying anything in the house, if a joiner or carpenter, you will have trouble in your family; and be careful of those who are working beside you.

Devil–To dream of this professed enemy to the human race denotes that many dangers will threaten you, all of which you will overcome.

Dice–To dream you are playing at dice or back gammon, denotes much good to the dreamer, in either love, marriage or trade.

Ditches–To dream of deep ditches, steep mountains, rocks, and other eminences, surely foretells danger and misfortune.

Doctor–To dream the doctor is in your house and attending some one sick, you will hear of some one unexpectedly and that they are doing well.

Dogs–To dream of these domestic and faithful animals, has very different significations, according to the manner in which you see them.

Drowning–To dream you are drowning, or that you see another drowned or drowning, portends good to the dreamer, to the lover it denotes that your sweetheart is good-tempered, and inclined to marry you.

Eagle–To dream you see an eagle soaring high, is a good omen to those who have great undertakings on hand; but to dream that an eagle alights upon us, signifies mischance.

Earthquakes–To dream of an earthquake, warns you that your affairs are about to take a very great change.

Eating–To dream you are eating, denotes profit and success in your present enterprise; a loathing of victuals, is a sign of disunion in your family.

Eel–To dream you see an eel in the water, if pure, is a good sign of plenty, and betokens good; if muddy water, bad.

Embracing–To dream you embrace without power to speak, denotes the party to fall in love, but shall not obtain the person desired.

Enjoyment–To dream you are enjoying yourself with your friends, betokens you to be very careful in what you are doing.

Eye-lash–To dream your eye-lash is red and sore, is sickness to yourself or to some of your friends.

Eyes–To dream you lose your eyes is a very unfavourable omen; it denotes decay of circumstances, loss of friends, death of relations, and miscarriage in love.–If a woman with child dreams of it, it denotes the child in her womb will be very unhappy, and before it arrives at years of maturity, lose its liberty.

Face–To dream that your face is swelled, shews that you will accumulate wealth; if you are in love, it denotes that your sweetheart will receive an unexpected legacy and marry.

Fall–To dream you fall from any high place, or from a tree, denotes loss of place and goods.

Feasting–To dream you are at a feast, denotes that you will meet with many disappointments, particularly in the thing which you are most anxious about.

Fields–To dream you are in green fields, is a very favourable sign.

Fighting–To dream you are fighting, denotes much opposition to your wishes; with loss of character and property.

Fire–To dream of fire, denotes health and happiness; to the lover, marriage with the object of the affections, and many children; also that you will be angry with some one for a trifle.

Fishing–To dream you are fishing, is a sign of sorrow and trouble.

Flowers–To dream you are gathering flowers, is a very favourable omen.

Flying–To dream you are flying, is a very excellent omen; it foretells elevation of fortune, that you will arrive at dignity in the state, and be happy.

Fortune–To dream you make a sudden fortune, is a bad omen.

Friend–To dream you see a friend dead, betokens hasty news, of a joyous nature; if you are in love, it foretells a speedy marriage with the object of your affection.

Fruit–Almonds indicate difficulties, loss of liberty, and deceit in love.

Funeral–To dream you are busily employed in burying a person, denotes a very speedy marriage, and that ere long you will hear of the death or imprisonment of some near relation or friend.

Gallows–To dream of the gallows is a most fortunate omen; it shows that the dreamer will become rich, and arrive at great honours.

Garden–To dream you are walking in a garden, denotes your advancement to fortune.

Geese–To dream of geese is a sign of good; you may expect to see an absent friend soon; to the dreamer, they denote successes and riches.

Gifts–To dream you have anything given to you, is a sign that some good is about to happen to you.

Glass–Denotes bad success in various undertakings; if you break it, it warns you of some unforeseen misfortune, and death of your wife, husband, or children.

Gold–If you dream of gold, it is a very good omen; it denotes success to your present undertaking, after encountering numerous difficulties.

Gooseberries–If growing on the bush, denote that you will have a numerous family, and great success in your present undertakings.

Grave–To dream of being buried is an omen, you will die very poor.

Guns–To see or hear guns firing denotes much misery; if you fire them, you will have a quarrel; if they are fired at you, you will be exposed to many dangers.

Hail–To dream of hail, denotes sorrow and much grief.

Hair–To dream that you are brushing or combing your hair, portends success in love, trade, or some other pursuit.

Hands–To dream of shaking hands, signifies to both sexes courtship and love.

Hanging–Dreaming that you see people hanged, or that you are to be executed yourself, is a sure sign that you will by marriage rise above your present position, or a favour will be asked by one in needy circumstances from you.

Hatred–Dreaming of being hated by friends or foes is a bad omen.

Hills–To dream of climbing up hills, shows that you will overcome many troubles, and at last die very rich.

Horses–To dream of horses, is very lucky; if you dream that you see white horses, they denote speedy news; if they are black, you may expect to hear of the death of an acquaintance.

House–To dream of building a house is a very favourable omen.

Hunting–To dream you are hunting a fox, and that he is killed, shows much trouble through the pretensions of false friends, but that you will discover them and overcome all their machinations.

Ice–To dream you are sliding or skating on ice, shows that you will be engaged in some imaginary pursuit that will elude you; if the ice breaks you may be certain of sickness.

Iron–To dream you are hurt with iron, shows you will receive some injury.

Keys–To dream you lose a key foreshadows anger, and that you will lose a friend.

Kissing–To dream that you kiss a pretty maid, indicates good; if she consents without any resistance, she will be true to her lover.

Knife–To dream you give a knife to your intended, shows you will lose him or her.

Ladder–To dream you climb a ladder, betokens a happy marriage and many children.

Lamb–To dream you feed or bring a young lamb to the slaughter, signifies torment; to dream you see a young lamb or kid, signifies extraordinary joy and comfort.

Letter–To dream of receiving a letter betokens a present; if you send one, you will relieve a person in bad circumstances.

Light–To see a light, is good; to strike a light, gain.

Lillies–A sign of a good marriage.

Linen–Some impediment to a journey; otherwise, luck.

Lion–To dream you see a lion, denotes the greatest prosperity and honour.

Looking-glass–Denotes nothing good, generally death.

Leaping–To dream you are leaping over anything, denotes you will fall into difficulties; it also shows crosses in love.

Lice–To dream of lice, is a sure sign of sickness; but if seen numerously, riches.

Mad–To dream of being mad, is very good; it promises long life, riches, a happy marriage, and good children.

Marriage–To dream you are married, signifies the death of yourself or some near relation; to dream you assist at a wedding, denotes pleasing news and great success; to dream of lying with your wife or husband, threatens sudden misfortunes and great danger.

Meat–To dream of raw meat, denotes trouble of a very severe description; if it is boiled, it betokens plenty of work to the tradesmen, and plenty to the family of the labourer; to the lover, a happy union.

Mice–To dream of mice, denotes success, love, and a happy marriage.

Milk–To dream you are selling milk, denotes that you will be crossed in love, that you will be unsuccessful in trade; to dream you are drinking of milk, is the forerunner of joyful news and great success.

Mines–To dig mines is a sign of hard work and little profit; to see mines fall in, signifies misfortune. To see a miner denotes some unexpected visit; to see miners work, betokens adversity.

Misery–To dream of being miserable, or to see misery in others, denotes disgrace and affliction.

Mixing–To dream of mixing liquors, denotes distress.

Money–To dream you are paying money, denotes success in your affairs; to see money, great joy; to receive as a present, good marriage; to collect, honour; to give, anger; to dream of having a good deal, denotes losses and sorrow; to find, unlucky; if you receive it, you will thrive in your undertakings.

Monk–Indicates crosses and vexation.

Monkies–Signifies sickness, but also great success in love; to see them dance is a favourable time to buy buildings.

Moon–When clear, gain; to imagine it looks fiery red, prosperity; with a halo, that you will be successful in play; pale, sickness; on the wane, riches; on the increase, poverty; under clouds, affliction.

Mother–Dreaming you see a mother is very fortunate; to see her dead is a sure sign of illness.

Mountains–To see mountains is a sign of great honour, esteem; to ascend, cares; to descend, that something unpleasant is about to happen to you.

Music–To hear music, sorrow.

Murder–Is a sign of long life; to imagine you see a murderer, good news.

Abraham Thornton. Tried for the murder of Mary Ashford

Maid–Dreaming of saluting a young girl, is vexation; to quarrel with one, a happy marriage.

Nails–To dream your nails are growing very long, is very good, and denotes riches, and great use to you.

Nakedness–To dream of nakedness, denotes scandal; if you see a naked female, it is lucky, it denotes that honour awaits you at no distant period.

Night–To dream you are travelling at night, foretells great vexation.

Nightingale–To dream of this pretty warbler, is the forerunner of joyful news, great success in business, of plentiful crops, and of a sweet tempered lover. For a married woman to dream of a nightingale, shows that she will have children who will be great singers.

Nose–Dreaming one has a fair and great nose, is good to all; for it implies subtilty of sense, providence in affairs, and acquaintance with great persons. But to dream one has no nose, means the contrary; and to a sick man, death.

Nosegays–To dream of gathering and making nosegays, is unlucky, showing that your best hopes shall wither as flowers do in a nosegay.

Nuts–Dreaming of gathering nuts, denotes that you will spend your time in pursuit of a trifling object, when you might employ it to better advantage.

Oak–If you see a stately oak, it is a sign of long life, riches, and great felicity.

Onions–To dream of onions, denotes that a mixture of good and bad will attend you. Your sweetheart will be faithful, but of a cross temper.

Oxen–If you dream that you see white oxen, it shows virtuous inclination; to see fat or lean oxen, signifies present gain and good fortune.

Old–Dreaming of seeing old men, is a sign you will be very fortunate. For a man to dream he is courting an old woman, and that she returns his love, is a very fortunate omen; it prefigures success in worldly concerns.

Oil–Dreaming you are anointed with oil, is very fortunate for women; but for men, it is ill, and implies shame.

Oven–To dream you see an oven, foretells that you are about to be separated from your family by changing your present residence.

Oysters–To dream of eating oysters, foretells prosperity, and that you will be married to a lady—a real virgin—who will love you.

Palm–To dream you are gathering of palm, denotes plenty, riches, and success in undertakings, and is a very good omen indeed.

Paper–To dream of paper, is a good omen, but if it appear crumpled, it will give you much pain.

Packages–Dreaming of packages, of any kind, forbodes uneasiness on account of children.

Pain–Dreaming you suffer pain, indicates gladness.

Path–To dream you are walking in an easy path, shows that you will be successful in love; or if you are married, you will obtain what you now wish for.

Paradise–To see paradise, is a sign of some joyful news.

Parents–To dream of seeing your parents, denotes prosperity and money.

Passage–Dreaming of a narrow passage, is riches.

Paying–Dreaming of paying a bill of fare, is vexation.

Peaches–Betokens friends.

Peacocks–To dream of seeing this beautiful bird is a very good omen; it denotes great success in trade.

Pears–If ripe, riches; unripe, adversity; to eat them good fortune.

Peas–Dreaming of peas well boiled, denotes good success.

Pigeons–To dream you see pigeons flying, imports hasty news of a pleasant nature, and great success in undertakings.

Pit–To dream you fall into a pit and cannot get out easily, denotes some serious calamity; that your sweetheart is false, and will prefer another. –To the sailor, shipwreck; to the farmer, a bad harvest.

Play–To dream you are at play, betokens great happiness in the married state, and increase of business.

Pond–To dream you see a pond with clear water in it, betokens great success in your undertakings.

Purse–To dream of finding a purse is a very favourable omen; in love, it is a sure token of a speedy marriage; to dream you lose your purse shows the loss of a friend.

Quarrel–If you dream you are quarrelling, it shows great happiness and contentment.

Queen–To dream you see the king and queen, signifies honour, joy, and much profit.

Racing–To dream you are running a race, is a token of good, presages much success in life, and that you will speedily hear some joyful news.

Rain–If you behold rain in your dream, it promises success in a love affair; and in all other respects it betokens trouble and vexation.

Rainbow–To dream you see a rainbow, it foretells sudden and great news.

Ravens or Crows–To dream you see a crow or raven, betokens great mischief; it shows falsehood in love.

Ribbon–To dream you wear ribbons, shows an entanglement in love to the single; and extravagant children to the married.

Riding–To dream you are riding, if it be with a woman, is very unfortunate; if you are in trade, business will decay; but if it be with men, then expect the reverse will happen, and you will obtain a sum of money by some speculation.

Rincing–To dream you rinced washed linen, is a sure sign of changing places.

Rings–To dream that you have a ring on your finger, denotes marriage to the person you love; but if the ring drop off it betokens death to a near friend.

River–Dreaming you see river water clear, indicates good; but to dream of swimming in the sea when it is muddy, signifies great peril and danger.

Rocks–A good dream for those going into business, as it shows great stability there.

Rods–To dream you are whipt with rods denotes that you will meet with a perfidious friend, who will go very near to ruin you; it also betokens your being shortly at a merry-making, where you must be careful of quarrelling; if you do, it will turn out to your disadvantage; in love it denotes your sweetheart to be of a fickle disposition, and little calculated to make you happy.

Roses–To the married, loss of their mate and children; to the lover, infidelity in his sweetheart.

Running–To dream you are running from the attack of any animal, is a sign that you will encounter great dangers, and that your lover will prove false.

Sea–To dream you are walking on the sea, is good for him who would take a wife, for he shall enjoy her.

Sailing–To dream you are sailing in a ship, and the water smooth, shows you will succeed in all your undertakings; if you sail in a small boat and gain the desired haven, you will gain great riches.

Shipwreck–To dream you are shipwrecked, the ship being overwhelmed and broken, is very bad, and shows that a supposed hatred of friends is groundless; live in peace with all mankind.

Sheep–To dream you are among sheep, means repose from trouble; to dream you meet a flock is lucky.

Shoes–To dream you have a pair of shoes, denotes success in life; in love matters, they signify marriage which will turn out an equal advantage to both parties.

Silk–To dream you are clothed in silk, signifies honour.

Silver–To dream of silver shows that you have got false friends, who will attempt your ruin; in love, it denotes that your sweetheart is false, and that he is engaged to another.

Snow–To dream that you see the ground covered with snow is good, to a young man it shows that he will marry a virgin, and have a large family.

Soldiers–To dream of soldiers, shows trouble, persecutions, and law suits; if they pursue you, it shows that you will be disliked by your rich neighbours.

Spit–To dream that you are in a kitchen turning a spit, is the forerunner of troubles and misfortunes; expect to be robbed, to lose your trade, or become very poor, and that your friends will desert you; if you are in love, it shows the object of your affections to be of a bad temper, lazy, and doomed to misfortunes and poverty.

Squirrel–To dream of a squirrel, shows that enemies are endeavouring to slander your reputation.

Starching–To dream you are starching of linen, shows you will be married to an industrious person, and that you will be successful in life, and save money; it also shows that you are about to receive a letter, containing some pleasant news.

Storms–To dream of storms and a troubled sky denotes that the person will get angry through the day.

Swans–To dream of seeing swans denotes happiness in the married state; and many children, who will become rich and respectable in your old age, with joy and happiness; to the lover, they denote constancy and affection in your sweetheart; in trade they show success, but much vexation from the disclosure of secrets.

Sun–To dream you see the sun shining, denotes accumulation of wealth; and filling high situations.

Swimming–To dream you are swimming with your head above the water, denotes great success in your undertakings, whether they be love, trade, sea, or farming. To dream of swimming with your head below the water, shows that you will experience some great trouble and hear some very unpleasant news from a person you thought dead. In trade it shows loss of business, and that you will perhaps be imprisoned for debt; in love it denotes disappointment in your wishes.

Teeth–To dream of losing your teeth, shows the loss of some friend by death, and that great trouble will accompany you.

Telegraph–To dream of the telegraph, denotes tidings from abroad, in a short space of time, and still the more speedily if you think the telegraph is at work.

Tempest–To dream that you are overtaken by a storm denotes that you will, after numberless hardships, arrive at happiness, and that you will become rich, and marry a good-natured lady.

Thunder and Lightning–To dream of thunder and lightning, denotes gain in your business; but if it hurts you, it is a sign of some calamity.

Toads–To dream you destroy a toad, denotes that you will discover a thief, in whom you placed great confidence.

Tree–To dream you see a withered tree sprouting out, denotes children in old age.

Trumpet–To dream you hear the sound of a trumpet, denotes troubles and misfortunes; to the lover, inconstancy in the object of his affection.

Water–To dream of drinking water, shows trouble and adversity; to the lover, it denotes that the pretensions of your sweetheart are false: he loves another and will never wed you.

Wedding–To dream of wedding is very unfavourable to lovers; it denotes sickness or death of some friend or relation.

Wheat–To dream you see, or are walking in a field of wheat, is a very favourable omen; and denotes great prosperity and riches; in love, it augurs a completion of your most sanguine wishes, and foretells much happiness, with fine children, when you marry; if you have a lawsuit, you will gain it, and you will be successful in all your undertakings.

Writing–When dreaming of writing a letter to your sweetheart, if you put it into the post, you will have a pleasing return; but to trust it into other hands, shows that your secrets will be exposed.

Wound–To dream you are wounded, denotes grief and vexation; if in the stomach or heart shows death.

11. The Supernatural

That way is by the gates of hell.
The Wife of Beith

Throughout the history of chapbooks and broadsides the supernatural had a considerable vogue, and some of the stories had an ancestry of several centuries. Not every tale whose title included words such as 'strange' or 'ghost' was necessarily a true anecdote of the other world— *The Ghost of my Uncle*, for example, which was a steady favourite over a long period, was simply an account of a practical joke played by an old man on his avaricious relatives. But *The Ghost of the Duke of Buckingham's Father* is in the orthodox tradition: the chapbook relates the appearance at Windsor Castle, on three occasions, of the ghost of Sir George Villiers (in armour) to an officer of the King's Wardrobe, warning him of the

Duke's being in danger of assassination if he did not take more heed of the people's feeling. Buckingham, fearless in battle, was soon after murdered at the age of thirty-six by a discontented subaltern, John Felton, in 1628.

Christopher Slaughterford, the hero of *The Guildford Ghost*, was executed at Guildford in Surrey on Saturday, 9th July 1709, for the murder of his mistress Jane Young. In spite of the very strong case put forward by the Crown, Slaughterford protested his innocence to the last, and many people claimed to have seen his ghost. The contemporary chapbook relates how he appeared to his manservant with a rope around his neck, a flaming torch in one hand and a club in the other, crying out for vengeance, while some of the prisoners in the Marshalsea swore that he rattled his chains there and terrified them once night had fallen. More dramatic was the legend of Madam Johnson, of *The Portsmouth Ghost*, described as 'a beautiful young lady of Portsmouth'. Seduced and abandoned by John Hunt, a captain in one of the regiments sent to Spain at the beginning of the eighteenth century, she sold herself to the devil. She then ripped herself open and flew off with the devil, leaving her unborn baby behind. On the captain's voyage back to England her ghost appeared to several of the sailors, who were soon told of her betrayal, and finally she carried John Hunt off into the night in a flame of fire:

> He went to turn and hide his face,
> She cry'd False man it is too late,
> She clasp'd him in her arms straightway,
> But no man knew his dying day.
> In a flash of fire many see
> She dragged him into the sea
> The storm is soon abated where
> They all returned thanks by prayer
> Unto the Lord that sav'd their lives
> And delivered them from that surprise
> Let this a warning be to all
> That reads the same both great and small.

Many tales sprang up around the famous Scottish covenanter, Alexander Peden (c. 1626–86), concerning his gift of second sight. Peden was ejected from his ministry in Galloway in 1662 and spent much of the rest of his life in hiding, sometimes in Scotland and at other times in Ireland. He was imprisoned for five years on the infamous Bass Rock. The chapbook that recounts his ability to prophesy the bloody events that befell both countries, does not hesitate to tell how he at one time lost confidence in his ability to foresee events:

Lads, I have lost my prospect wherewith I was wont to look over to the bloody land, and tell you and others what enemies and friends were doing; the devil and I puddles and rides time-about upon one another; but if I were uppermost again, I shall ride hard, and spurgaw well.

When he was near to death he returned to his birthplace and hid in a cave. It was on this occasion that he made his most famous prophecy:

1. That God shall make Scotland a desolation.
2. There shall be a remnant in the land, whom God should spare and hide.
3. They should lie in holes and caves of the earth, and be supplied with meat and drink: And when they come out of their holes, they shall not have freedom to walk, for stumbling on the dead corpses.
4. A stone cut of a mountain, should come down, and God shall be avenged on the great ones of the earth, and the inhabitants of the land, for their wickedness, and then the church should come forth with a bonny bairn-time of young ones at her back.

Peden said that if he were buried only once, these things might not come to pass, but if he were buried more than once, they would happen. Two days later he died and was buried in the Laird of Affleck's Isle. But the English troops heard of his death, dug up his corpse and reburied it at the foot of Cumnock-gallows. His friends later put a gravestone above his remains:

Here Lies
MR. ALEXANDER PEDEN
A Faithful Minister of the Gospel,
at Glenluce,
Who departed this life January 28, 1686,
And was raised after six weeks
Out of his Grave,
And buried here out of contempt.

Witchcraft and magic were very much part of people's lives during the earlier years of the chapbooks. One of the most popular of the legends was the story of Friar Bacon, which bore little resemblance to that of the real Roger Bacon (c. 1214–92), the 'doctor mirabilis'. As an inventor of the magnifying-glass and as an experimenter in the properties of gunpowder, Bacon had a reputation even during his lifetime of possessing more than human skills, and this grew rapidly after his death. The chapbooks made of him not only a magician but also a practical joker, as in the tale of his man Miles. Miles, a simple man, was unable to comply with his master's strict observance of fast days and kept a private reserve by him to tide him over the worst moments. On Good Friday, the strictest of all fast days, Bacon put a spell on him when he was secretly eating, so the monks found Miles, with a pudding stuck in his mouth, tied to the college gate, with the following inscription on his back:

This is Friar Bacon's man, who vow'd to fast,
But, dissembling, thus took it at last;
The pudding more religion had than he;
Though he would eat it, it will not down, you see.
Then of hypocrisy pray all beware,
Lest like disgrace be each dissembler's share.

More ingenious is the tale of Bacon's rescuing a young man who had sold himself to the devil. The young man had been tricked into signing in blood that, when he had repaid all his debts with the money the devil had given him, he would surrender himself to the devil and be disposed of at his pleasure. In desperation he appealed to Bacon for help, and the devil was persuaded to submit the case to the wily friar's judgment. When Bacon had heard both sides of the story he asked the young man if he had repaid the devil any of the money he owed him. 'No,' he replied, 'not one farthing.' 'Why then,' said Bacon, 'Mr. Devil, his debts are not discharged; you are his principal creditor, and according to this writing, can lay no claim to him until every one of his debts are discharged.' Furious, the devil disappeared in a flame, raising a mighty tempest about him.

The best thing about the widely circulated chapbook called *Satan's Invisible World Discovered* is its title and the dramatically depicted face of a terrified man on the cover. The contents comprise the rather dreary tale of Major Thomas Weir and his sister who were executed for witchcraft in 1676; the matter-of-fact story of the murder of a maidservant; and an account of the haunting of Woodstock Manor. The one interesting feature of this book is that all three events are set in the seventeenth century: their continuing popularity in the first half of the nineteenth century indicates the strange hold that these hoary anecdotes maintained on a more sophisticated population. A more lively tale is *The Miracle of Miracles* in which a young woman, Sarah Smith of Darken in Essex, who was very disobedient to her parents and 'was mightily given to Wishing, Cursing and Swearing,' gave birth to a monster:

the Body of it like a Fish with Scales thereon: it had no Legs but a pair of great Claws, Tallons like a Liands, it had six heads on its Neck, one was like the Face of a Man with Eyes Nose and Mouth to it, the 2d like the Face of a Cammel, and its Ears Cropt, Two other Faces like Dragons with spiked Tongues hanging out of their Mouths, another had an Eagles

Head with a Beak instead of a Mouth at the end of it, and the last seeming to be a Claves head. Which eat and fed for some time, which Monster has surprised many Thousand people that come there to see it.

By the command of the magistrates, the unfortunate monster was eventually knocked on the head—which one?—and it was dissected in the interests of science. The supercilious reader who felt any doubt concerning the truth of the story was assured that it would be 'certify'd by the Minister and Church-Wardens of the said Parish'. To add to its verisimilitude, the story is further embellished by a very engaging woodcut portrait of the monster with all six heads plainly depicted.

The Wonder of Wonders, the tale of a sailor, John Robinson, is of unusual interest since it includes a conversation with a mermaid, which gives fair warning that it is wise for mortals to ensure that they have the first word in such encounters:

> to his great Amazement, he espy'd a beautiful young Lady combing her head, and toss'd on the Billows, cloathed all in green (but by chance he got the first word with her) then she with a Smile came on board [the abandoned ship] and asked how he did. The young Man being Something Smart and a Scholar, reply'd Madam I am the better to see you in good Health, in great hopes trusting you will be a comfort and assistance to me in this my low Condition; and so caught hold of her Comb and Green Girdle that was about her Waist. To which she replied, Sir, you ought not to rob a young Woman of her Riches, and then expect a favor at her Hands; but if you will give me my Comb and Girdle again, what lies in my power, I will do for you.

This he did and, in return, the mermaid gave him a compass and he was able to return home safely. Unfortunately, the next time he saw the mermaid she spoke first and thus rendered him dumb. She promised to come to see him again, but she never did, and in a short time he pined away and died 'to the wonderful Admiration of all People who saw the young Man'.

12. Superstitions

Nature sometimes in her roughest coat drops her brightest jewel
The True Fortune Teller

Superstitions have a way of surviving when all else changes. One of the signs by which the little fortune-telling books all set great store was the significance of the position of moles on different parts of the body. On the neck a mole promised future riches, while on the lower part of the neck it ensured marriage as well. A mole on the left breast threatened poverty, ill-fortune and 'the displeasure of superiors'; on the right breast, however, it betokened riches and prosperity—but if it was right in the middle of the chest it indicated a person of cruel and sullen disposition. Not only the position of the mole, but sometimes its colour as well, had a bearing on its meaning.

Nails, too, could indicate to the initiated a great deal about a person's character. Broad nails betokened people of gentle disposition; but certain white marks at the end testified that the person would soon ruin his fortune through improvidence. A man with narrow nails was desirous of attaining knowledge in the sciences, but was never long at peace with his neighbours. If his nails were long as well, he would be led away by ambitious desires, aiming at things which he could not obtain. Round nails declared a hasty person, yet good-natured, and very forgiving—a lover of knowledge, doing no one any harm, and acting according to his own imagination, being rather too proud of his own abilities.

One of the strangest things was the concoction of the Dumb Cake which, in order to make to perfection, it was necessary to observe strictly the following instructions:

Let any number of young women take a handful of wheaten flour (not a word is to be spoken by any one of them during the rest of the process) and place it on a sheet of white paper; then sprinkle it over with as much salt as can be held between the finger and the thumb; then one of the damsels must bestow as much of her own water as will make it into a dough; which, being done, each of the company must roll it up, and spread it thin and broad, and each person must (at some distance from each other) make the first letters of her christian and surname, with a large new pin, towards the end of the cake; if more christian names than one, the first letter of each must be made. The cake must then be set before the fire, and each person must sit down in a chair, as far distant from the fire as the room will admit, not speaking a single word all the time. This must be done soon after eleven at night; and between that and twelve, each person must turn the cake once, and in a few minutes after the clock strikes twelve, the husband of her who is first to be married will appear, and lay his hand on that part of the cake which is marked with her name.

Other superstitions covered a remarkable area: to cut one's nails on Sunday was unlucky, and on Wednesday prognosticated a quarrel—Monday was the best day, other days being of no significance. If a pair of bellows was found lying on a table or on the floor, it was a sign of words in the domestic circle. If they were put behind the door, it showed trouble for debt; but laid on a chair, it denoted the near approach of a welcome stranger to the house. Burning beef bones brought sorrow through poverty; casting pork or veal bones on the fire inflicted pains in the bones of so impoverished a person; and burning fish or poultry bones engendered scandal on the consumer, especially if it was a woman. Cutting hair in Passion Week, or on a Wednesday or Sunday was unlucky. It was very unlucky to stumble when on the road to the church to get married; it denoted early separation, or widowhood. To meet a funeral while on the road to church for one's wedding showed that the future held a life of domestic jars, and a very indifferent partner. It was a certain sign of dissension or unpleasantness or unhappy tidings from a distant quarter, if a fire burnt black and gloomy. If the fire spat or roared, it indicated some heavy displeasure from a superior or from someone who had authority over one.

Various editions of Mother Bunch's soothsayings were current for at least two, and possibly three, centuries. The legendary Mother Bunch hailed from 'Bonny Venter in the West', and the books bearing her name clearly were the repository of many very ancient superstitions. Mother Bunch specialized in telling young people how to find out whom they were going to marry:

But hark you! daughter, I have had three husbands myself, and I think to have another yet, and do you think I am so mad to tell him all that I do? no I am not so mad and I think thou wilt be a little wiser and yet daughter, I have another way for to teach thee how thou shalt come to know who must be thy husband, and I have approved it true; for I tryed it myself, and now is the best time of the year to try it, and therefore take notice of what I say: Take a St. Thomas onion, and peel it, and lay it in a clean handkerchief and lay it under your head; and put on a clean smock, and be sure the room be clean swept where you lye, and as soon as you be laid down, be sure lay thy arms abroad, and say these words:

> Good St. Thomas do me right,
> And bring my love to me this night,
> That I may look him in the face,
> And in my arms may him embrace.

Then lying on thy back, with thy arms abroad, fall asleep as soon as thou can, and in thy first sleep thou shalt dream of him which shall be thy husband, and he will come and offer to kiss thee, but do not hinder him but strive to catch him in thy arms, and if thou do get hold of him that is he which must be thy husband but if thou get not hold of him thou must try another night, and if thou do get hold of him hold him fast, for that is he. This I have try'd, and it has prov'd true. Yet I have another pretty way for a maid to know her sweetheart, which is as followeth: Take a summer apple, of the best fruit you can get, and take three of the best pins you can get, and stick them into the apple close to the head, and as you stick them in take notice which of them is in the middle, and what name thou fancies best give that middle pin and put it into thy left handed glove, and lay it under thy pillow on a Saturday at night, but thou must be in bed before thou lays it under thy head, and when thou hast done, clasp thy hands together, speaking these words:—

> If thou be he that must have me
> To be thy wedded bride,
> Make no delay, but come away,
> This night to my bedside.

And in thy first sleep thou shalt see him come in his shirt and lie down by thee, and if he offer thee any abuse it will be a great sign he will prove one that will love other women as well as thee; but if he do put his hand over thee to imbrace thee be not afraid of him, for it is a great sign he will prove a good husband; and this is a good way for a young man to know his sweetheart, giving the middlemost pin the name he fancies best, putting an apple in his right handed glove, and lay it under his pillow, when he is in bed, saying,

> If thou be she that must have me
> In wedlock for to join,
> Make no delay but come away
> Unto this bed of mine.

And that night he shall see her come, and if she come in her smock and petticoat, which is a great sign she will prove a very civil woman; but if she come without her petticoat there is danger she will prove a ranter, and therefore better lost than won.

The most charming of all the different counsels Mother Bunch offered was for St Valentine's Day, 14th February, 'at which time the fowls of the air begin to couple'. Mother Bunch told young women to take five bay leaves, lay one under every corner of the pillow and the fifth in the middle. Then, when they lay down, to repeat these lines seven times over:

> Sweet Guardian Angel let me have
> What I most earnestly do crave
> A Valentine endow'd with love,
> That will both kind and constant prove.

13. Riddles

New Riddles make both Wit and Mirth
The Price of a Penny, yet not half the Worth.

Riddles are an integral part of the heritage of every nation: they help to throw light on the interests and preoccupations of its people, and on its cultural and commercial links with other nations. Most riddles of any worth have a lengthy history, and it is amusing to recognize in some contemporary examples the skilful adaptation of conundrums that appeared to be already old when the Greeks were consulting the Sphinx. During the long night of revelry at which the Pindar of Wakefield's men vied with Robin Hood's band in providing entertainment, it was inevitable that some riddles should be included:

What is that which is fittest for the body when life is out?
Some said a grave; others, a winding-sheet. No, said another, *a hot caudle and a warm bed is fittest for a woman newly delivered.*

What is it that hangs, bears, and blows not?
A porridge pot.

Red beat black on the belly, and made her belly rumble?
Fire under a pot making it seethe.

A man and his wife fell at strife for an undone deed. Up steps the good man and stops the hole that open was, and then they were agreed?
They fell out about the stopping of the oven.

There dwels a shoemaker by this hall,
That makes his shoes without an awl,
Though men of them they do not wear,
Yet of them they buy many a pair?
A smith making shoes for horses.

154

I am no viper, yet I feed
On mother's breasts, that did me breed,
I sought a husband, in which labour
I found out the kindness in a father,
He is father, husband, brother, too;
Who this may be, resolve it you.
>   *One that married her own father.*

There was a man bespoke a thing,
The which another did him bring,
He that made it did refuse it,
He that bespoke it would not use it,
And he that us'd it did not know,
Whether he us'd it aye or no?
>   *A coffin for a dead man.*

The riddles in the later chapbooks were not as obscure as some of the Pindar's. One of the most pleasing of the collections in this form was *A Whetstone for Dull Wits; or, A Poesy of New and Ingenious Riddles,* which included:

Into this world I came hanging,
>   And when from the same I was ganging,
I was cruelly batter'd and Squeez'd,
>   And men with my blood, they were pleased?
>   *It is a Pipping pounded into Cyder.*

A Wide Mouth, no ears nor eyes,
No scorching flames I feel—
Swallow more than may suffice
Full forty at a meal.
>   *It is an Oven.*

Tho' of great age
I'm kept in a Cage
Having a long tail and one ear,
My mouth it is round
And when Joys do abound
O' then I sing wonderful clear.
>   *It is a Bell in a Steeple; the Rope betokens a
>   Tail, and the Wheel an ear.*

The greatest travellers that e'er were known
>   By Sea and land were mighty archers twain;
No armor proof, or fenced walls of stone,
>   Could turn their arrows; bulwarks were in vain.

Thro' princes courts, and kingdoms far and near,
    As well in foreign parts as Christendom,
These travellers their weary steps then steer,
    But to the deserts seldom come.
        'Tis Death and Cupid, whose arrows pierce thro' the
        Walls of Brass or strong Armour in all Courts and
        Kingdoms in the habitable World.

Two Calves and an Ape
They made their escape
From one that was worse than a spright;
They travell'd together
In all sorts of weather
But often were put in a fright.
        'Tis a Man flying from his scolding wife; the two
        Calves and an Ape, signify the calves of the legs and
        the Nape of his neck, which by travelling was
        expos'd to the weather.

A thing with a thundering breech
It weighing a thousand welly,
    I have heard it roar
    Louder than Guys would boar,
They say it hath death in its belly,
    It is a Cannon.

It flies without wings,
Between silken strings
And leaves as you'll find
It's guts still behind.
    It is a Weaver's Shuttle.

Close in a cage a bird I'll keep,
That sings both day and night,
When other birds are fast asleep
It's notes yield sweet delight.
    It is a Clock.

To the green wood
Full oft it hath gang'd,
Yet yields us no good
Till decently hang'd.
    It is a hog fattened with Acorns, which makes good
    bacon when hanged adrying.

Rich, yellow, and bright,
Long, slender and white,

Both one in another there are;
Now tell unto me,
What this Riddle may be,
Then will I your wisdom declare.
    A Diamond ring on a Lady's finger.

A Visage fair
And voice is rare,
Affording pleasant charms;
Which is with us
Most ominous
Presaging future harms.
    A Mermaid, which betokens destruction to Mariners.

To ease men or their care
I do both rend and tear
Their mother's bowels still;
Yet tho' I do,
There are but few
That seem to take it ill.
    'Tis a Plough which breaks up the bowels of the
    Earth for the sowing of Corn.

My back is broad, my belly is thin,
And I am sent to pleasure youth;
Where mortal man has never been
Tho' strange it is a naked truth.
    A Paper Kite which mounts the lofty air.

By sparks in lawn fine
I am lustily drawn,
But not in a chariot or Coach;
I fly, in a word,
More swift than a bird,
That does the green forest approach.
    An Arrow drawn in a Bow by a Gentleman Archer.

By the help of a guide
I often divide
What once in a green forest stood;
Behold me, tho' I
Have got but one eye,
When that is stopt I do the most good.
    A Hatchet, with which they cleave Wood; till the
    Eye is stopped with the Haft, it cannot perform business.

Q. Two Calves and an Ape / They made their escape / From one that was worse / than a spright; They travell'd together / In all sorts of weather / But often were put in a fright.

A. *'Tis a Man flying from his scolding wife; the two Calves and an Ape, signify the calves of the legs and the Nape of his neck, which by travelling was expos'd to the weather.*

Q. A thing with a thundering breech / It weighing a thousand welly, / I have heard it roar / Louder than Guys wild boar, / They say it hath death in its belly.

A. *It is a Cannon.*

Q. My weapon is exceeding keen, / Of which I think I well may boast, / And I'll encounter Colonel Green / Together with his mighty host. / With me they could not then compare, / I conquer them both great and small, / Tho' thousands stood before me there / I stood and got no harm at all.

A. *A Man mowing of Grass with a Scyth, which took all before it.*

Question. Into this world I came hanging, / And when from the same I was ganging, / I was cruelly batter'd and Squeez'd, / And men with my blood, they were pleas'd.

Answer. *It is a Pipping pounded into Cyder.*

Q. By sparks in lawn fine / I am lustily drawn, / But not in a chariot or / Coach; I fly, in a word, / More swift than a bird, / That does the green force approach.

A. *An Arrow drawn in a Bow by a Gentleman Archer.*

Q. By the help of a guide / I often divide / What once in a green forest / stood; Behold me, tho' I / Have got but one eye, / When that is stopt I do the / most good.

A. *A Hatchet, with which they cleave Wood; till the Eye is stopped with the Haft, it cannot perform business.*

Q. Once hairy scenter did transgress, / Whose dame, both powerful and fierce, / Tho' hairy scenter took delight / To do the thing both fair and right, / Upon a Sabbath day.

A. *An old Woman whipping her Cat for Catching Mice on a Sunday.*

Q. Close in a cage a bird I'll keep, / That sings both day and night, / When other birds are fast asleep / It's notes yield sweet delight.

A. *It is a Clock.*

Q. To the green wood   Yet yields us no good
   Full oft it hath gang'd,   Till decently hang'd.

A. *It is a hog fattened with Acorns, which makes good bacon
when hanged a drying.*

Q. Rich, yellow, and bright,   Now tell unto me,
   Long, slender and white,   What this Riddle may be,
   Both one in another there   Then will I your wisdom
   are ;   declare.

A. *A Diamond ring on a Lady's finger.*

Q. There was a sight near Charing Cross,
   A creature almost like a horse ;
   But when I came the beast to see,
   The head was where the Tail should be.

A. *A Mare tied with her tail to the Manger.*

Q. Tho' of great age   My mouth it is round
   I'm kept in a Cage   And when Joys do abound
   Having a long tail and one   O' then I sing wonderful clear.
   ear,

A. *It is a Bell in a Steeple; the Rope betokens a Tail, & the
Wheel an ear.*

Q. A Visage fair   Which is with us
   And voice is rare,   Most ominous
   Affording pleasant charms ;   Presaging future harms.

A. *A Mermaid, which betokens destruction to Mariners.*

Q. To ease men of their care   Yet tho' I do,
   I do both rend and tear   There are but few
   Their mother's bowels still ;   That seem to take it ill.

A. *'Tis a Plough which breaks up the bowels of the Earth for
the sowing of Corn.*

Q. Tho' it be cold I wear no cloaths,
   The frost and snow I never fear,
   I value neither shoes nor hose,
   And yet I wander far and near ;
   Both meat and drink are always free,
   I drink no cyder, mum, nor beer,
   What Providence doth send to me
   I neither buy, nor sell, nor lack.

A. *A Herring swimming in the Sea.*

Q. It flies without wings,   And leaves as you'll find
   Between silken strings   It's guts still behind.

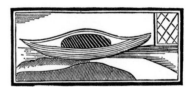

A. *It is a Weaver's Shuttle.*

Another delightful collection of riddles is *The True Trial of Understanding; or, Wit Newly Reviv'd. Being a Book of Riddles Adorned with Variety of Pictures*. It included the following:

> Tho' it be cold I wear no cloaths,
> The frost and snow I never fear,
> I value neither shoe nor hose,
> And yet I wander far and near;
> Both meat and drink are always free,
> I drink no cyder, mum, nor beer,
> What Providence doth send to me
> I neither buy, nor sell, nor lack.
> > *A Herring swimming in the Sea.*

> Once hairy scenter did transgress,
> Whose dame both powerful and fierce,
> Tho' hairy scenter took delight
> To do the thing both fair and right,
> Upon a Sabbath day.
> > *An old Woman whipping her Cat for Catching Mice on a Sunday.*

> There is a steeple standing fair,
> 'Tis built upon a rock of care,
> Therein a noise both fierce and shrill,
> Tho' here was neither clock nor bell.
> > *An old Woman scolding in a high crown'd Hat.*

> Promotion lately was bestow'd
> Upon a person mean and small;
> Then many persons to him flow'd,
> Yet he return'd no thanks at all;
> But yet their hands were ready still
> To help him with their kind good will.
> > *It is a Man pelted in the Pillory.*

> There was a sight near Charing Cross,
> A creature almost like a horse;
> But when I came the beast to see,
> The head was where the Tail should be.
> > *A Mare tied with her tail to the Manger.*

> As I walk'd thro' the street,
> It was near twelve o'clock at night;
> Two all in black I chanc'd to meet,
> Their eyes like flaming fire bright.

They passed by, and nothing said,
Therefore I was not much afraid.
> *Two long lighted Links carried along the street.*

Three men near the flowing Thames,
Much pains and labour did they take
They did both scratch and claw their wems,
Until their very hearts did ache.
It is as true as e'er was told,
Therefore this riddle now unfold.
> *Three Fidlers in Thames Street, who played up a bridegroom in the Morning, who gave them nothing to drink.*

My weapon is exceeding keen,
Of which I think I well may boast,
And I'll encounter Colonel Green
Together with his mighty host.
With me they could not then compare,
I conquer them both great and small,
Tho' thousand stood before me there
I stood and got no harm at all.
> *A Man mowing of Grass with a Scyth, which took all before it.*

I saw five birds all in a cage,
Each bird had but one single wing,
They were an hundred years of age,
And yet did fly and sweetly sing.
The wonder did my mind possess,
When I beheld their age and strength;
Besides, as near as I can guess,—
Their tails were thirty feet in length.
> *A Peel of Bells in a Steeple.*

Dougal Graham was also known as 'John Cheap' and as 'John Falkirk'. Under the latter name he contributed to the growing number of riddle-books with his *John Falkirk's Cariches*. There are just over ninety 'cariches' in this little chapbook and, like everything else that Graham wrote, they are original and entertaining. Some of the more interesting riddles are:

Q. What time of the year is it that there are most holes open?
A. In harvest when there are stubbles.

Q. Who was the goodman's muckle cow's calf's mother?
A. The muckle cow herself.

Q. How many sticks gangs to the digging of a craw's nest?
A. None, for they are all carried.

Q. Where did Moses go when he was full fifteen years old?
A. Into his sixteenth.

Q. What is the reason the dogs are worst on chapmen than on any other strangers?
A. It is said, the dogs have three accusations against the chapman, which has been handed down from father to son, or from one generation of dogs to another; the first is as old as Æsop, the great wit of Babylon.—The dogs having a lawsuit against the cats, they gained the plea: one of the dogs coming trudging home with the Decreet below his tail, a wicked chapman threw his ell-wan at him, and he let the Decreet fall and so lost their great privileges thereby. The second is, because in old times the chapman used to buy dogs and kill them for their skins. The third reason is, when a chapman was quartered at a farmer's house, that night the Dog lost his right of licking the pot.

Q. Amongst what sort of creatures will you observe most of a natural law, or instinctive knowledge?
A. The Hart and the Hind meet on one certain day in the year; the Brood Goose lays her first egg on Eastern's Even, old stile; the Crows begin to build their nest about the first of March old stile; the Swans observe matrimony, and if a female die, the male dares not take up with another or the rest will put him to death; all the Birds in general join in pairs and keep so; but the Dove resembles the adulterer, when the hen grow old he puts her away and takes another; the Locusts observe military order, and march in bands; the Frogs resemble gipsies and pedlers, for the young ones ride the old ones to death.

Q. What are the vainest sort of people in the world?
A. A Barber, a Tailor, a young Soldier, and a poor dominie.

Q. What is the great cause of the barber's vanity?
A. Because he is admitted to trim Noblemen's chafts, thake their sculls, take Kings by the nose, and hold a razor to their very throats, which no other subject dare presume to do.

Q. What is the great cause of the Tailor's pride?
A. His making of peoples new clothes, of which every person, young and old is proud. Then who can walk in a vainer show than a tailor carrying home a gentleman's new clothes?

Q. What is the cause of a young Soldier's pride?
A. When he lists, he thinks he is free of his mother's correction, the hard usage of a bad master, his liberty to curse, swear, whore, and do every thing, until he be convinced by four halberts and the

drummer's whip, that he has now got both a civil and military law above his head, and, perhaps, far worse masters than ever.

Q. What is the cause of the poor dominie's pride?

A. As he is the teacher of the young and ignorant, he supposes no man knows what he knows; and because boys call him master, therefore he thinks himself a great man.

Q. What is the reason that young people are vain, giddy-headed and airy, and not so obedient as the children of former years?

A. Because they are brought up and educated after a more haughty strain, by reading fables, plays, novels, and romances; gospel books, such as the Psalm-book, Proverbs, and Catechisms, are like old almanacks; there is nothing in vogue but fiddle, flute, Troy and Babylonish tunes; our plain English speech is corrupted with beauish cants, such as dont, wont, nen, and ken; a jargon worse than the Yorkshire dialect or the Hottentot gibberish.

Q. Why is swearing become so common among Scottish people?

A. Because so many lofty teachers came from the south amongst us, where swearing is practised in its true grammatical perfection! Hot oaths, new struck, hath as bright a lustre as a new quarter guinea just come from the mint.

Q. What are the two things not to be spared, but not to be abused?

A. A soldier's coat and a hired horse.

Q. How is a man in debt like a nobleman?

A. Because he has many to wait on and call for him.

Q. How is swearing like a shabby coat?

A. Because it is a bad habit.

Q. Why is a drawn tooth like a thing that is forgot?

A. Because it is out of one's head.

Q. Who are the two greatest thieves in Great Britain?

A. Tea and Tobacco, for they pick the pockets of the whole nation.

Q. Who is likest to a Boatman?

A. An hypocrite, who always looks one way and rows another, in all his transactions.

Q. What are the five greatest rarities to be found in the world?

A. A black Swan, a Phoenix, an Unicorn, the Philosopher's Stone, and a maiden at sixteen.

Q. Who has the honestest trade in the world?

A. Ballad-singers; for they always deal with ready-money: and it is as ancient as the Siege of Troy, for Homer was a ballad-singer.

Q. What is the wisest course to be followed by a man who has a brawling and scolding wife?

A. To keep silent, and then she'll bite her own fingers with anger.

Q. What thing is that which is lengthened by being cut at both ends?

A. A ditch.

Q. What is that which was born without a soul, lived and had a soul, yet died without a soul?

A. The whale that swallowed Jona.

Q. What is the longest and the shortest thing in the world? the swiftest and the slowest? the most indivisible and the most extended? the least valued and the most regretted? without which nothing can be done? which devours all that is small, yet gives life and spirit to all that is great?

A. Time.

Q. What creatures are those which appear closely connected, yet upon examination are found to be three distinct bodies, with eight legs, five on one side, and three on the other; three mouths, two straight forwards, and the third on one side; six eyes, four on one side, two on the other; six ears, four on one side, and two on the other?

A. A Man and Woman on horseback [the woman riding side-saddle].

Q. Why is a churchyard like an inn?

A. Because it receives weary travellers.

Q. Why is a carrotty lady like a troop of soldiers?

A. Because she bears fire-locks.

Q. What did Adam first set in the garden of Eden?

A. His foot.

Q. How is it that a clergyman's horse is like a King?

A. Because he is guided by a minister.

Q.   What kind of snuff is that, the more that is taken the fuller the box is?

A.   It is the snuff off a candle.

Q.   What relation is that child to its own father who is not its father's own son?

A.   Surely his daughter.

Q.   What is that which is often brought to the table, always cut, but never eaten?

A.   A pack of cards.

Q.   Why is a brewer's horse like a tap-ster?
A.   Because they draw drafts of drink.

Q.   How many toads' tails will it take to reach up to the moon?
A.   One, if it be long enough.

Q.   What is the best method of catching rogues?
A.   There is none so fit as a rogue himself.

Glossary

Aceldama   scene of slaughter

Bag the swag   pocket someone's watch-chain and seals

Bellman   public-crier

Blate   rave, talk wildly

Blawflum   nonsense, a hoax

Bools   curved handles

Brock   badger

Caller   fresh, newly-caught

Canting crew   beggars

Carich   (literally) catechism

Chafts   jaws, jawbones

Civileers   inquisitors appointed conjointly by the town council and the kirk session

Codlin   a kind of apple

Croppies   Irish rebels of 1798 who sympathized with the French revolution

Cummer   woman

Cwot   coat

Daddle   fist

Draw the fogles plummy   steal people's handkerchiefs adroitly

Dubsman   turnkey in a jail

Duke   duck

Dummy   pocket-wallet

Ell-wan   measuring rod

Flee   fly

Flyting   wrangling, tirade

Fork the rag   steal money

Frisk the cly   pick someone's pocket

Gomeral   simpleton, fool

Gowl   howl, cry

Ground sweat   grave

Jags   scraps

Jasey   worsted head-covering resembling a wig

Kiddy is my famble   so expert is my technique

Kilmainham   one of Dublin's jails

Lanthorn   lantern

Link   torch

Links and basils   chains, and fetters on one leg only

Mappen   temporarily

Muckle   full-grown

Nubbling chit   gallows

Padders on the high way   highwaymen

Patterer   vendor of street literature who sang the ballads and read the broadsheets

Pinder   official in charge of the cattle pound

Puddles   tramps through the mud

166

Rumbler   hackney-coach; tumbril

Skellat Bellman   public crier (a skellat was a small bell carried by the public crier)

Skillygolee   thin gruel

Soom   swim

Speak to the tattler   steal someone's watch

Spurgaw   to dig in one's spurs

Sweat their duds   pawn their clothes

Taffety   tender, delicate

Thake   thatch

Tip the deck   deal the cards

Trepan   entrap, decoy

Voider   a large open basket; a clothes-basket; a small finely-made wicker basket

Wem   belly

Reading List

American broadsides, prints and maps. Philadelphia, The Rosenbach Company, 1949. 68 pages.

Ashbee, Edmund William, *editor. Occasional fac-simile reprints of rare and curious tracts of the sixteenth and seventeenth centuries.* London, the editor, 1868–72. 2 volumes.

   Includes some chap-books.

Ashton, John, *editor. A century of ballads.* London, Elliot Stock, 1887. xx, 354 pages.

Ashton, John. *Chap-books of the eighteenth century, with facsimiles, notes, and introduction.* London, Chatto and Windus, 1882. (Reprinted Bronx, N.Y., Benjamin Blom, 1966.) xvi, 486 pages.

   Most of the favourite traditional stories—Guy of Warwick, Dr Faustus, Friar Bacon, etc.—some in full, others in brief. Profusely illustrated with the original woodcuts.

Ashton, John. *Modern street ballads.* London, Chatto and Windus, 1888. (Reprinted Detroit, Singing Tree Press, 1967.)

Attention pioneers! San Francisco, Book Club of California, 1952. (Keepsake series, no. 15.)

   Facsimile reproductions of twelve rare California broadsides or posters, 1847–96. With explanatory comment by various authorities.

Baildon, William Paley. *A catalogue of pamphlets, tracts, proclamations, speeches, sermons, trials, petitions from 1506 to 1700, in the Library of the Honourable Society of Lincoln's Inn.* London, Lincoln's Inn, 1908. xii, 482 pages.

Berger, Carl. *Broadsides and bayonets; the propaganda war of the American Revolution.* Philadelphia, University of Pennsylvania Press, 1961. 256 pages.

Berry, W. Turner *and* Buday, George. 'Nineteenth-century broadsheets.' *The Penrose Annual*, volume 49, 1955, pages 28–30.

Bland, Desmond Sparling. *Chapbooks and garlands in the Robert White Collection.* Newcastle upon Tyne, King's College Library, 1956. 32 pages.

Bloom, James Harvey. *A calendar of broadsides and single sheets relating to the county of Suffolk.* 1921. 16 pages.

Bloom, James Harvey. *English tracts, pamphlets and printed sheets [1473–1650]: a bibliography.* London, W. Gandy, 1922. 2 volumes.
Includes facsimiles.

Catalogue of prints and drawings in the British Museum. Division I: Political and personal satires. London, British Museum, 1870 to date.

Catalogue of the Lauriston Castle chapbooks in the National Library of Edinburgh. Boston, Mass., G. K. Hall, 1965. 273 pages.
Over four thousand entries for chapbooks published during the 17th, 18th and—principally—19th centuries in various parts of Britain.

Cheney, C. R., 'Early Banbury chapbooks and broadsides'. *The Library*, volume 17, 1936–7, pages 98–108.

The Chronicle of the Gitelson Kamaiko Foundation, New York, no. 1, 1964.
Issue includes 'American colonial broadsides, 1527–1653'; 'English, German, and French proclamations, 1514–1848'; 'English polemical pamphlets, 1612–1677'; 'Portuguese Brazilian proclamations, c. 1500–1550'.

Collier, John Payne, *editor. Broadside black-letter ballads, printed in the sixteenth and seventeenth centuries.* London, printed for private circulation by T. Richards, 1868. xii, 120 pages. (Reprinted: New York, Burt Franklin, 1968.)
Illustrated by original woodcuts.

Collier, John Payne, *compiler. Broadsides of speeches, songs, etc., delivered in the presence of General Monck, chiefly in the halls of public companies of London, just anterior to the Restoration.* London, the compiler, 1863. iv, 40 pages. (Illustrations of early English popular literature, volume 2, no. 6.)

Collmann, Herbert Leonard, *editor. Ballads and broadsides, chiefly of the Elizabethan period and printed in black-letters.* Oxford, the University Press for the Roxburghe Club, 1912. xiii, 287 pages.
Most of the items had been in the Heber Collection before being acquired by the Britwell Court Library.

Colum, Padriac, *editor. Broad-sheet ballads: being a collection of Irish popular songs.* Dublin and London, Maunsel, 1913. 76 pages.

The comic songster. 2nd edition. Glasgow, W. Hamilton, 1939–40. 2 volumes.
Includes chapbooks.

Crawhall, Joseph, *editor. Olde tayles newlye relayted.* London, The Leadenhall Press. 1883. 444 pages.

Croker, T. Crofton, *compiler. The popular songs of Ireland.* London, Henry Colburn, 1839. xx, 340 pages.

Cropper, Percy James. *The Nottinghamshire printed chap-books, with notices of their printers and vendors.* Nottingham, Frank Murray, 1892. xi, 32 pages.

Cunningham, Robert Hays, *editor. Amusing prose chap-books, chiefly of the last century.* London, Hamilton, Adams; Glasgow, Thomas D. Morison, 1889. 350 pages.

> The text—but no illustrations—of a number of favourites: *Wise Men of Gotham*; *Thomas Hickathrift*; *Jack the Giant-Killer*; etc.

Curious old Scottish religious works; or, The popular theological chap literature of the last century. Glasgow, Lindsay.

De Vries, Leonard. *Flowers of delight.* London, Dobson, 1965.

Draper, John William, *editor. A century of broadside elegies, being ninety English and ten Scotch broadsides illustrating the biography and manners of the seventeenth century.* London, Ingpen and Grant, 1928. xviii, 229 pages.

> Facsimile reprints.

Edmond, John Philip, *compiler. Bibliotheca Lindesiana: catalogue of English broadsides, 1505–1897.* Aberdeen, the University Press, 1898. xl, 526 pages.

An exhibition of street literature. London, St Bride Foundation, Printing Library, 1954. 8 pages.

An exhibition of street literature from the collection of John Foreman, Eric Swift, and Toni Savage. Leicester, College of Art and Design, Faculty of Teacher Training, 1968.

Fawcett, Frank Burlington, *editor. Broadside ballads of the Restoration period.* London, John Lane, 1930. xxvi, 248 pages.

> Ninety-three ballads from the Jersey Collection known as the Osterley Park ballads.

Federer, Charles A., *editor. Yorkshire chap-books. First series: comprising Thomas Gent's tracts on legendary subjects: with a memoir of the author, and a select number of facsimiles reproductions of the original woodcuts.* London, Elliot Stock, 1889. 280 pages.

> Includes: *St. Winefred*; *Christ and the Apostles*; *Judas Iscariot*; *Job*; *St. Robert of Knaresborough.*

Field, Louise Frances. 'Some chapbooks, and the progress of the spelling-book', in her *The Child and his book.* 2nd edition. London, W. Gardner, Darton, 1892.

Ford, Worthington Chauncey. *Broadsides, ballads, etc., printed in Massachusetts, 1639–1800.* Boston, The Massachusetts Historical Society, 1922. xvi, 483 pages (Collections: volume 75).

Fraser, John, *The humorous chap-books of Scotland.* New York, Henry L. Hinton; Glasgow, James Hadden, 1873–4. 2 parts.

> The third part, 'Simple prose narratives', was never published. The Life of Dougal Graham (Part II, pages 157–218) is especially worth reading.

A garland of new songs. Newcastle-upon-Tyne, J. Marshall, c. 1800. 3 volumes.

Garret, William, *compiler. A right pleasant and famous book of histories.* Newcastle-upon-Tyne, the compiler, 1818. 5 volumes.

Gerring, Charles. *Notes on printers and booksellers, with a chapter on chap books.* London, Simpkin, Marshall, 1900. viii, 118 pages.

Golding, Charles, *editor. Suffolk scarce tracts, 1595 to 1684.* Norwich, the author, 1873. 31 pages.

Gomme, Sir George Laurence, and Wheatley, Henry Benjamin, *editors. Chapbooks and folk-lore tracts.* First series. London, printed for the Villon Society, 1885. 5 volumes.
 Includes Tom Hickathrift: The Seven wise masters of Rome; Mother Bunch; Patient Grisel; Dick Whittington.

Graham, Dougal. *The collected writings of Dougal Graham, 'Skellat' Bellman of Glasgow.* Edited with notes, together with a biographical and bibliographical introduction, and a sketch of the chap literature of Scotland, by George MacGregor. Glasgow, T. D. Morison, 1883. 2 volumes.
 Includes many chapbooks.

Halliwell-Phillipps, James Orchard, *compiler. A catalogue of chapbooks, garlands, and popular histories.* London, the compiler, 1849. (Reprinted Detroit, Singing Tree Press, 1968.)

Halliwell-Phillipps, James Orchard, *compiler. A catalogue of proclamations, broadsides, ballads, and poems, presented to the Chetham Library, Manchester.* London, C. and J. Adlard, 1851. xx, 272 pages.

Harvey, William. *Scottish chapbook literature.* Paisley, Alexander Gardner, 1903. 155 pages.
 Includes sketches (pages 36–64) of the 'Skellat Bellman of Glasgow', Dougal Graham (c. 1724–79), and William Cameron (1781–1851) of Stirling.

Hazlitt, William Carew, *editor. Shakespeare jest-books: reprints of the early and very rare jest-books supposed to have been used by Shakespeare.* London, Willis and Sotheran, 1864. 3 volumes. (Old English jest-books.)

Healy, James N., *editor. The Mercier book of old Irish street ballads.* Cork, The Mercier Press, 1967–71. 3 volumes.

Heartman, Charles Frederick, *compiler. The cradle of the United States, 1765–1789: a collection of contemporary broadsides, pamphlets, and a few books pertaining to the history of the Stamp Act; the Boston massacre, and other pre-revolutionary troubles; the War for Independence, and the adoption of the Federal Constitution.* Metuchen, N.J., the compiler, 1922–3. 2 volumes.

Henderson, William, *editor. Victorian street ballads: a selection of popular ballads sold in the street in the nineteenth century.* London, Country Life, 1937. 160 pages.

Hindley, Charles. *The Catnach Press: a collection of the books and woodcuts of James Catnach, late of Seven Dials, printer.* London, Reeves and Turner, 1869.

Hindley, Charles. *Curiosities of street literature: comprising 'cocks,' squibs, histories, comic tales in prose and verse*. London, Reeves and Turner, 1871. (Reprinted London, 'The Broadsheet King', 1966.) 265 pages.

Hindley, Charles. *The history of the Catnach Press, at Berwick-upon-Tweed, Alnwick, and Newcastle-upon-Tyne, in Northumberland; and Seven Dials*. London, Charles Hindley the younger, 1887. (Reprinted Detroit, Singing Tree Press, 1968.) xlii, 308 pages.

Hindley, Charles. *The life and time of James Catnach (late of Seven Dials), ballad monger*. London, Reeves and Turner, 1878. xvi, 432 pages. (Reprinted Detroit, Singing Tree Press, 1968).

Includes 230 woodcuts, of which 42 are by Bewick.

Hindley, Charles, editor. *The old book collector's miscellany; or, A collection of readable reprints of literary rarities, illustrative of the history, literature, manners, and biography of the English nation during the sixteenth and seventeenth centuries*. London, Reeves and Turner, 1871–3. 3 volumes. (Miscellanea antiqua anglicana.)

Hodgkin, John Eliot. 'English broadsides' in his *Rariora*, volume III. London, S. Low, Marston, 1902.

Holloway, John. 'Cherry girls and crafty maidens'; 'Broadside verse traditions'; 'The Irish ballads'. *The Listener*, volume 83, 21 May; 28 May; 4 June, 1970, pages 680–5, 710–14, 744–8, respectively.

A brilliant and important series of three articles on the later English broadside ballads. Includes texts of a number of unusual and well-written ballads.

Ingleton, Geoffrey Chapman, editor. *True patriots all; or, News from early Australia, as told in a collection of broadsides*. Sydney, Angus and Robertson, 1952. 380 pages.

Jantz, Harold Stein. 'Unrecorded verse broadsides of seventeenth-century New England'. *Papers* of the Bibliographical Society of America, volume 39, 1945, pages 1–19.

Includes facsimiles.

John Cheap, the chapman's library: the Scottish chap literature of last century, classified. With life of Dougal Graham. Glasgow, Robert Lindsay, 1877–8. 3 vols. (Reprinted Detroit, Singing Tree Press, 1969.)

Jones, Redvers, editor. *The Life of old Jemmy Catnach, printer*. Newlyn, Penzance, The Craft Press, 1965. vii, 12 pages.

Klingberg, Frank Joseph, and Hustvedt, Sigurd Bernhard, editors. *The warning drum: the British home front faces Napoleon: broadsides of 1803*. Berkeley and Los Angeles, University of California Press, 1944. vii, 287 pages.

Based on the collection of the William Andrews Clark Memorial Library of the University of California at Los Angeles.

Laws, George Malcolm. *American balladry from British broadsides: a guide for students and collectors of traditional song*. Philadelphia, American Folklore Society, 1957. xiii, 315 pages. (Bibliographical and special series, volume 8.)

Lemon, Robert, *compiler. Catalogue of a collection of printed broadsides in the possession of the Society of Antiquaries of London.* London, Society of Antiquaries, 1866. xi, 228 pages.

Lilly, Joseph, *editor. A collection of seventy-nine black-letter ballads and broadsides, printed in the reign of Queen Elizabeth, between the years 1559 and 1597.* London, Lilly, 1867. xxxvi, 319 pages. (Reprinted Detroit, Singing Tree Press, 1968.)

M'Bain, James M., *compiler. Bibliography of Arbroath periodical literature and political broadsides.* Arbroath, Brodie and Salmond, 1889. 128 pages.

McMurtrie, Douglas Crawford. *Some Massachusetts broadsides of 1711.* Metuchen, N.J., the author, 1934. 18 pages.

The magazine of history, with notes and queries. Extra numbers 1–200 (volumes 1–50). Tarrytown, N.Y., W. Abbatt, 1908–35.
    Includes reprints of broadsides and proclamations.

Muir, Percy H. *Catnachery.* San Francisco, The Book Club of California, 1955. 27 pages.

The National Union Catalog: pre-1956 imprints. Volume 103. London, Mansell, 1970, pages 401–6.
    These pages give a vast amount of bibliographical information concerning copies of British and American chapbooks mostly in the Library of Congress.

Neuberg, Victor Edward. *Chapbooks: a bibliography of references to English and American chapbook literature of the eighteenth and nineteenth centuries.* London, The Vine Press, 1964. 88 pages.

Neuberg, Victor Edward. *The penny histories: a study of chapbooks for young readers over two centuries.* London, Oxford University Press, 1968; New York, Harcourt, Brace, 1969. [viii], 227 pages. (Milestones in children's literature.)
    History of production of chapbooks in Britain and the USA (pages 1–77). Includes full facsimile reproductions of seven chapbooks: *Guy of Warwick*; *Fairy stories*; *The Children in the Wood*; *Cock Robin*; *Nations of the World*; *Toads and Diamonds*; *The Rod.*

Neuberg, Victor Edward, *compiler. A select handlist of references to chapbook literature of the eighteenth and nineteenth centuries.* Edinburgh, the compiler, 1952. 28 pages.

O'Lochlainn, Colm, *editor. Irish street ballads.* Fontwell, Sussex, Centaur Press, 1960.

Pearson, Edwin. *Banbury chap books and nursery toy book literature (of the XVIII and early XIX centuries.)* London, A. Reader, 1890. (Reprinted New York, Burt Franklin, 1972.) 116 pages.
    Many illustrations by the Bewicks, Blake, Cruikshank, Craig, Lee, Austin, etc.

Ratcliffe, F. W., 'Chapbooks with Scottish imprints in the Robert White Collection'. *The Bibliotheck*, volume IV, nos. 3 and 4, 1964.

Ritchie, James T. R. *The singing street*. Edinburgh, Oliver and Boyd, 1964. 140 pages.

Rollins, Hyder Edwards, *editor. Cavalier and Puritan: ballads and broadsides illustrating the period of the great rebellion, 1640–1660*. New York, The New York University Press, 1923. xv, 532 pages.

Rollins, Hyder Edwards, *editor. The pack of Autolycus; or, Strange and terrible news of ghosts, apparitions, monstrous births, showers of wheat, judgments of God, and other prodigious and fearful happening as told in broadside ballads of the years 1624–1693*. Cambridge, Mass., Harvard University Press, 1927. xvii, 269 pages.

Rollins, Hyder Edwards, *editor. A Pepysian garland:* [80] *black-letter broadside ballads of the year 1595–1639, chiefly from the collection of Samuel Pepys*. Cambridge, the University Press, 1922. xxxi, 490 pages.

Rosner, Charles, *compiler, The writing on the wall, 1813–1943*. London, Nicholson and Watson, 1943. 48 pages.

Thirty-eight items from the Napoleonic collection of broadsheets, cartoons and prints bequeathed by the Marquess Curzon to Oxford University. Arranged to illustrate the invasion threat directed against Britain in 1708–1803; Napoleon's 1812–13 campaign in Russia; his Egyptian venture to open the road to India in 1799; and, the 'United Nations' of 1813.

Rudolph, Earle Leighton. *Confederate broadside verse: a bibliography and a finding list*. New Braunfels, Texas, The Book Farm, 1950. 118 pages. (Heartman's historical series, no. 76.)
Includes two facsimiles.

Rye, Reginald Arthur. *Catalogue of the collection of broadsides in the [London] University Library*. 1928. 201 pages.
Supplement. 1930. 4 pages.

Shaabar, Matthias Adam. *Some forerunners of the newspaper in England, 1476–1622*. Philadelphia, University of Pennsylvania Press, 1929. xi, 368 pages.
Includes facsimiles of broadsides.

Shepard, Leslie. *The broadside ballad: a study in origins and meaning*. London, Herbert Jenkins, 1962. 205 pages.

Shepard, Leslie. *John Pitts, ballad printer of Seven Dials, London, 1765–1844; with a short account of his predecessors in the ballad and chapbook trade*. London, Private Libraries Association, 1969. 160 pages.

The history of ballads, broadsheets and chapbooks from earliest times to the nineteenth century (pages 13–95). Reproductions of outstanding items (pages 97–121). Bibliographical appendices.

Singer, Samuel Weller, *editor. Shakespeare's jest book*. London, Chiswick Press, 1814–15. 2 parts.
Supplement. 1815, 28 pages.

Spinney, Gordon Harold. 'Cheap repository tracts: Hazard and Martin edition'. *The Library*, 4th series, volume XX, no. 3, 1939, pages 295–340.

Thomson, Frances Mary, *compiler. Newcastle chapbooks in Newcastle upon Tyne University Library: a catalogue.* Newcastle upon Tyne, Oriel Press, 1969. 109 pages.

Introduction includes details concerning thirteen local producers of chapbooks. The catalogue lists the contents of 614 chapbooks. Indexes of titles, imprints, and authors. Seven woodcuts.

Tuer, Andrew White. *Pages and pictures from forgotten children's books.* London, Leadenhall Press, New York, Scribner, 1898–9. 510 pages.

Includes facsimiles.

University of Kentucky collection of English chap books. Lexington, University of Kentucky Library, 1952. 21 pages. (Occasional contributions, no. 34.)

Weiss, Harry Bischoff. *American chapbooks.* Trenton, N.J., the author, 1938, 31 pages.

Includes facsimiles.

Weiss, Harry Bischoff. *American chapbooks, 1722–1842.* New York, New York Public Library, 1945, 19 pages.

Weiss, Harry Bischoff. *A book about chap-books, the people's literature of bygone times.* Trenton, N.J., Edwards Brothers, 1942. (Reprinted Philadelphia, Pa., Folklore Associates, 1969.) v, 149 pages.

Weiss, Harry Bischoff, *compiler. A catalog of the chap-books in the New York Public Library.* New York, The New York Public Library, 1936. 90 pages.

Includes facsimiles.

Welsh, Charles *and* Tillinghast, William Hopkins. *A catalogue of [2,461] English and American chapbooks and broadside ballads in Harvard College Library.* Cambridge, Mass., Harvard University Library, 1905. (Reprinted Detroit, Singing Tree Press, 1968.) xi, 171 pages.

Winship, George Parker. *Brown University broadsides.* Providence, R.I., 1913, 7 pages.

Winslow, Ola Elizabeth. *American broadside verse from imprints of the 17th and 18th centuries.* New Haven, Conn., Yale University Press, 1930. xxvi, 224 pages.

Includes facsimiles of broadsides.

Wolf, Edwin, *compiler. American song sheets, slip ballads and poetical broadsides, 1850–1870: a catalog of the collection of the Library Company of Philadelphia.* Philadelphia, The Library Company, 1963. 205 pages.

Includes facsimiles.

Index